DESSERTS

that have killed better men than me

Also by Jeremy Jackson
The Cornbread Book

Jeremy Jackson

that have killed better men than me

a sweet tooth's most wanted recipes

WILLIAM MORROW

An Imprint of HarperCollins*Publishers*

HarperCollins books may be purchased for educational, business, or sales promotional use. For information please write: Special Markets Department, HarperCollins Publishers Inc., 10 East 53rd Street, New York, NY 10022.

FIRST EDITION

Designed by Leah Carlson-Stanisic

Printed on acid-free paper

Library of Congress Cataloging-in-Publication Data

Jackson, Jeremy, 1973-
    Desserts that have killed better men than me / Jeremy Jackson.
        p.   cm.
    ISBN 0-06-052712-9 (hc.)
    1. Desserts.   I. Title.

    TX773.J33 2004
    641.8'6—dc21

                                                    2003048825

04 05 06 07 08 WBC/QW 10 9 8 7 6 5 4 3 2 1

for my sisters

contents

Frozen Desserts   91

Uncategorizable Desserts   103

Basic Recipes   115

acknowledgments

For support and inspiration, I'm grateful to Elizabeth and Paul Luce, Harriet Bell, David Dunton, Harvey Klinger, Kelly Smith, and my parents.

In addition, I thank Gypsy Lovett, Rebecca Shapiro, Kate Stark, and Carrie Bachman for their hard work on my behalf.

Also, the joke in the introduction about looking like a just-released prisoner in a suit is my uncle Jim's joke, and I stole it without even asking permission, and I feel terrible about the whole thing.

KitchenAid was most generous in supplying me with excellent equipment. And I thank Cuisinart for sending me a terrific ice cream maker.

INTRODUCTION

Toward a Dessert Cosmology

n the beginning, there was sugar. And also butter. And they were good, and if you beat them together until they reached a fluffy, aerated consistency, it was called "creaming," which was odd because cream hadn't even been discovered yet. Which was very odd, because how could you make butter without cream? Go figure.

The point being: whoever invented dessert was a genius. But that's another topic for another time.

About the Title

When I was working on my first cookbook, *The Cornbread Book*, I was constantly inventing titles for cookbooks that I might write someday. In part, this was a coping technique designed to distract me from the fact that I was slightly weary of eating cornbread every day for months on end. Most of the cookbook titles I came up with were useless, like *My Damn Meat Loaf, Desserts You Can Mail,* and

The Scratch and Sniff Cookbook. But one title, *Desserts That Have Killed Better Men Than Me*, struck me immediately as being fantastically great. Or greatly fantastic. Either way, I recognized that it was a title that deserved an actual book to go with it. In other words, it was *bookworthy*. Which was very convenient, since I just happened to be a writer and a recipe developer.

"Well," I said to myself, "*I could write that book. I could write Desserts That Have Killed Better Men Than Me.*"

"Pipe down," my girlfriend said.

"And I like desserts!" I said. "I really, really like desserts!"

"You think you're talking to yourself," my girlfriend said. "But really you're talking out loud and I can hear everything you're saying."

It was true. So I had to continue my conversation with myself at a later time, while the girlfriend was in the shower.

But in thinking about writing *Desserts That Have Killed Better Men Than Me*, I quickly ran into a problem. To wit: I am not a very good man. I do not, for example, own a pair of black shoes. And if you put me in a suit, I look like a man who has just been released from prison and was issued a suit. Also, I have not held a full-time job since I was twenty, unless you count moping or hypochondria. Or the internet. Or catalog shopping. Anyway, enough said.

Who, I wondered, would want to read a book about desserts that have killed better men than me when, well, the *standard* set by the title was so low?

But then I realized that though the admission that I am not a very good man is embarrassing, it, in fact, worked to my advantage. For if I were a significantly better man, that would mean that the range and number of excellent desserts that have killed better men than me would be much narrower and boring. Perhaps such a selection of desserts would make for a good pamphlet, but not an entire cookbook. So luckily, I am not a very good man.

The other problem with the title was the verb tense. These would be desserts that *had* killed, not *might, should, could,* or *would* kill. In other words, the title implied that desserts contained therein had an actual track record of being so good that they were deadly. But I didn't want to write a book that contained only classic desserts that were tried and true. I wanted to develop new recipes. And I didn't want to alter the title at all. My solution: leave the title alone, go ahead and develop new recipes, and put one measly paragraph about the whole mess in the introduction, thus protecting myself from critics by pointing out the semantic imprecision myself. Ha!

On the Matter of Health

Of course, the real truth behind my punch-line title is that desserts, by and large, aren't the healthiest things you can eat. But I believe there is room for the occasional decadent dessert in a healthy diet. Don't hate me for saying this, but while I was writing *Desserts That Have Killed Better Men Than Me,* I lost five pounds. I lost this five pounds because I exercised regularly and I ate carefully—even though I did have to eat desserts every day.

In the end, I think, it comes down to two factors: frequency and portion size. Don't eat rich desserts every day. And eat small portions. Julia Child has always said, "Everything in moderation." Those are words to live by.

But not all of the desserts in this book are artery cloggers. I've included a list of low- and no-fat desserts in the Dessert Finder section on page 133.

A Glimpse of My Dessert-Impoverished Childhood

I didn't taste refined sugar until I was nineteen. Okay, that's not true. But that's what it *seemed* like. My mother regularly served fruit for dessert. Fruit! My position, growing up, was that fruit is not a dessert. I have now changed my mind on that matter, but at the time it was a horrible injustice I suffered through.

My mother was also rather famous for making chocolate chip cookies with whole wheat flour. She also decreased the sugar in the recipe. Not only that, but she would reduce the number of chips by such a drastic amount that it was not uncommon to get a cookie that had *no* chips in it. What's up with that? A cookie with two chips was about as good as it got. On occasion, we would find a cookie with three chips in it. In such an instance, fights broke out. Punches were thrown.

This is a lesson: good and plentiful desserts keep the peace.

A Word About Selectivity

Title aside, what I really wanted to write was a book filled with recipes that were all knockouts. I didn't want to settle on any dessert that wasn't sublime. I'm tired of so-so recipes in books and magazines. It's as if there's a huge recipe-writing computer out there churning out these recycled, rehashed recipes over and over. When I look at the typical cookbook, I know that about half of the recipes are so-so, a quarter are decent, and only the final quarter— if you're lucky—are worth making. I just don't have the time or inclination to figure out which of the recipes are the great ones. I want all the recipes to be great. Is that too much to ask? There's just no room for mediocrity in the wonderful world of desserts. I mean, if we wanted mediocrity, we'd just settle for store-bought cookies and all those horrible recipes that include almond bark. What is almond bark anyway? Well, it's evil, I think.

Who are these people who write cookbooks with 700 recipes in them? Or 1,000 recipes? Or 1,500 recipes? What amphetamines are these people on? Do they truly develop and test all these recipes? Are all these recipes sensational? I don't think so.

So instead of presenting you, the reading and eating public, with a dessert book that has a couple hundred slightly-better-than-average recipes, I present you with a book that has sixty-something fantastic recipes in it—some of which are somewhat familiar, some of which are novel, but all of which are sublime. I stand behind them all, each and every one. Plus, this book will take up less space on your shelf. And it will cost less than a book with 200 recipes. And I promise that there's no almond bark in it. Just plenty of heavy cream.

INGREDIENTS

··

there's no way around it: great desserts are born of great ingredients. Fresh, high-quality ingredients are the baker's best friend and can even help compensate for the occasional mistake. That said, bakers are lucky in that their most essential ingredients are usually pantry staples like flour, sugar, and eggs. Chances are you could make many of the recipes in this book with the ingredients you have on hand right now.

But baking also relies on precision. If bread flour is substituted for cake flour in a cake recipe, the cake will fail. And if unsweetened chocolate is used when bittersweet chocolate is called for, well, tears will fall. And so on and so forth. True, there are many acceptable ingredient substitutions—and a good baking reference book like Regan Daley's *In the Sweet Kitchen* will help you make appropriate substitutions—but if you want the recipe to turn out right, stick to the details.

Sugar When using granulated sugar, I prefer cane sugar. Unless a sugar is clearly labeled as cane sugar, it is probably beet sugar.

Dark and light brown sugars are generally interchangeable in recipes, though I prefer light brown sugar, as my recipes indicate. Brown sugar should always be packed into the measuring cup for accuracy.

Flour   In developing most of the recipes in this book, I used Gold Medal all-purpose flour. You can expect similar results with any national-brand all-purpose flour or unbleached all-purpose flour. Regional all-purpose flours, such as White Lily or King Arthur unbleached all-purpose flours, are not recommended here because of their different protein contents.

In the recipes that call for cake flour, any national-brand cake flour will work.

Eggs   All my recipes call for large eggs. It's not a good idea to substitute another size of egg. Eggs can usually be kept for about a week past the date stamped on the carton, but only if they're stored in a cold part of the refrigerator instead of the warm on-door egg tray that many refrigerators have. Organic eggs generally have a better flavor than factory-farm commercial eggs.

Milk and Cream   I developed all the recipes in this book using 2 percent milk. In general, you can substitute other kinds of milk, but results may vary.

I use organic pasteurized heavy cream whenever possible. Compared to the ultrapasteurized cream found in most supermarkets, organic pasteurized cream has significantly better flavor. After all, if you're going to indulge in something as decadent as heavy cream, why not go for the best? Look for organic cream in a good natural foods store or, increasingly, in the dairy section of your supermarket.

Note that heavy cream is sometimes labeled "heavy whipping cream."

Butter   All my recipes call for unsalted butter, which is generally fresher than salted butter. Unsalted butter also allows the baker to control the amount of salt in any given recipe—and, of course, many dessert recipes contain no salt at all. Salted butter contains approximately ¼ teaspoon of salt per stick (8 tablespoons). If you must use salted butter in one of my recipes, reduce the salt in the recipe accordingly.

When "creaming" butter and sugar—an integral part of many cookie and cake recipes—it's important that the butter be at room temperature. The easiest thing to do is to let the butter come to room temperature by letting it sit on your counter until it's just right—assuming, of course, that the temperature in your kitchen is between about 67 and 72 degrees.

A way to speed up the warming process is to cut the butter into slices, so that there is more surface area. An even faster method is to grate the butter with a cheese grater, which can bring the butter to room temperature in 10 or 15 minutes. It's a bit messy, but it works.

In a pinch, a microwave can be used to bring butter to room temperature, but you have to be extremely careful not to overheat the butter. Cut the butter into half-tablespoon slices and arrange the slices upright on a saucer or in a small bowl. Microwave the butter for a few seconds, then pause for several seconds. Repeat this cycle, checking the temperature of the butter frequently. At the first sign of melting, you must stop. Ideally, the butter will be at room temperature before any part of it has started to melt.

Vanilla Extract and Vanilla Beans   Pure vanilla extract is worth every penny. One excellent brand is Nielsen-Massey, available in well-stocked supermarkets and from sources like Williams-Sonoma and The Baker's Catalogue (see Sources, page 137). Never, ever, use artificial vanilla flavoring.

Vanilla beans may also seem like a decadent purchase, but they add so much flavor to custards and ice creams and other desserts. There's truly no substitution. Many of the vanilla beans I see in supermarkets are small, dried out, and overpriced. It's better to get your vanilla beans from a reputable source, such as Penzeys Spices (see Sources, page 137). Store your vanilla beans in an airtight container in a cool, dark place—but not in the refrigerator, which is too moist.

Chocolate It's easy to confuse the many categories of chocolate, and such confusion can ruin a recipe. When dealing with chocolate, read the recipe carefully and make sure you're using the right kind of chocolate.

Bittersweet chocolate is the kind of chocolate most commonly used in this book. It is lightly sweetened. Sometimes it's labeled "dark chocolate." There is a wide variety of flavors and sweetness levels within the realm of bittersweet chocolate, so you should experiment and find your favorites. Though premium brands such as Scharffen Berger, Lindt, Valrhona, Callebaut, and Ghirardelli are excellent chocolates, there are also some bargains to be had. Hershey's Special Dark is a great baking chocolate, and you can find it everywhere—in your drugstore or supermarket's candy aisle, for example. I'm also very fond of the reasonably priced Merckens bittersweet chocolate, which is available from The Baker's Catalogue (see Sources, page 137).

Semisweet chocolate has more sugar in it than bittersweet chocolate, though there is no official dividing line between the two. In general, it's acceptable to substitute semisweet chocolate for bittersweet chocolate, though the chocolate flavor will be less pronounced. Note: semisweet chocolate chips are formulated for use in cookies, and they should not be substituted for any other kind of chocolate.

Unsweetened chocolate, sometimes called baking chocolate, has no sugar in it. You can find it in the baking aisle of your supermarket, but I generally find the mass-market unsweetened chocolates to be subpar. A good professional-quality (but reasonably priced) unsweetened chocolate like Callebaut is preferable. You can buy Callebaut's unsweetened chocolate from Sweet Celebrations (see Sources, page 137).

When buying white chocolate, make sure there are no fillers, such as vegetable oil, on the ingredients list. Make sure it contains cocoa butter.

Store all chocolate in a cool, dry place.

Fruit   In nearly all instances, fresh local in-season produce has more and better flavor and will improve your recipes. If it happens to be organic produce, all the better. Look for local produce markets and orchards in your phone book. Frequent your local farmers' market.

Citrus Zest   The zest of a citrus fruit is the thin, oil-rich outer layer of the skin. It is the part of the skin that is colored. Beneath this layer is the white pith, which is generally bitter. Thus, the idea in removing the zest from a piece of citrus fruit is to remove the colored layer without disturbing the pith. To accomplish this, one can employ a citrus zester, a Microplane grater, or even the small holes on a good all-purpose grater. When you're using citrus fruit for its zest, use organic fruit if possible in order to avoid the pesticides and waxes common on commercial fruit. If you can't use organic fruit, wash the citrus fruit in warm water and mild dishwashing soap before zesting. If the recipe you're following also calls for juice from the same fruit you're zesting, remove the zest first, then juice it—it's almost impossible to do it the other way around.

Nuts   Instead of paying too much for tiny packages of half-rancid nuts at the supermarket, buy your nuts from a good bulk food store or natural foods store with high turnover. Store nuts in airtight containers in the freezer for up to four months.

EQUIPMENT

....

Like good ingredients, good tools are vital to your success in the kitchen. It's certainly not always necessary to own the most expensive equipment available, but it is important to be educated. I'm not going to list every piece of equipment you need—I'll assume you have some decent knives, pans, cutting boards, spatulas, etc.—but there are a few things I want to point out.

Ovens   Your biggest ally—or, if your oven isn't up to snuff, your biggest foe. A remarkable number of home ovens have thermostats that aren't correctly calibrated. If your oven is running as little as 10 degrees hotter or cooler than it indicates, your recipes will suffer. Do yourself a favor and buy a good oven thermometer. If your oven is running hot or cold, you can compensate for it or have your thermostat professionally recalibrated.

Many ovens also have hot and cold spots. Ever notice that when you pull a batch of cookies out of the oven that the cookies in one corner of the baking sheet are overdone while the cookies in the opposite corner are underdone? Well, the simple solution is to rotate your baking sheet in the oven—top to bottom, front to back—halfway through the baking time.

Professional bakers make a lot of fuss about which position the oven rack should be in for a certain recipe. It does make a difference, but for the home baker, I think it's perfectly fine to leave a rack somewhere between one-third and one-half of the distance from the bottom of the oven. With a couple of exceptions, I developed all the recipes in this book using that oven rack position.

For best results, preheat your oven for at least 15 minutes. And never bake more than one item or baking sheet at a time unless the recipe says you can. Notable exceptions to this rule are pies, cakes, and tarts—which can generally be baked in pairs.

Mixers A countertop stand mixer is a powerful tool, and it can make short work of creaming butter or whipping up some egg whites. It is especially useful when something needs to be mixed for a long period of time. But in most instances a good hand-held mixer can achieve the same results. When it comes to mixers, quality counts. The first hand mixer I ever bought burned out the first time I used it. KitchenAid is a trustworthy brand.

Food Processors and Blenders Again, quality counts. Both of these appliances can save you much time and frustration.

Baking Pans The primary thing to keep in mind when considering baking pans is that they will affect the end product. For example, a dark cookie sheet will brown the bottoms of cookies much faster than a light cookie sheet. For this reason, I tend to avoid dark baking pans. If you want a nonstick pan, look for one with a light gray coating, as opposed to a darker coating. I bake many cookies and cakes on parchment paper anyway, so I don't have much need for nonstick baking pans. And when buying baking pans, thicker, heavier construction is usually preferable.

Parchment Paper and Silicone Sheets   If you haven't discovered the wonderful properties of parchment paper, you should give it a try. This paper makes any pan nonstick, allowing cookies and cakes to slide easily from their pans. And the paper can be reused if it's not too dirty. You can find parchment paper in many supermarkets, any professional baking supply store, or through mail-order companies like The Baker's Catalogue (see Sources, page 137). The quality of parchment paper does vary—find a sturdy brand that works for you.

Rubberized silicone baking mats sold under brand names like Silpat and Exopat also make any baking sheet nonstick. They can be washed and reused for years. They're downright amazing.

Scale   For some recipes, a good scale, preferably digital, is essential for measuring ingredients accurately.

Measuring Cups   For accuracy, dry ingredients should always be measured in graduated dry-ingredient measuring cups, and wet ingredients should always be measured in a see-through liquid measuring cup.

For accuracy when measuring flour, I employ the dip-and-sweep method: dip the measure into the flour; sweep off the excess with the straight edge of a knife for a level measure.

Pie Plates   For some reason, a lot of home cooks have strange ideas about which pie plates produce the best crust, the most even baking, etc. In my experience, the ubiquitous and inexpensive Pyrex pie plate is the hands-down winner in all categories. And the glass lets you see how brown the bottom of the crust is!

Double Boiler   I've encountered a lot of confusion about double boilers. But an understanding of them is vital, especially when making ice cream.

A double boiler is a pot within a pot—nothing more, nothing less.

But there's really no need to go out and buy a double boiler. A good metal bowl set atop a saucepan containing about an inch of simmering water is just as good. The only thing to keep in mind is that the bottom of the bowl should *never* touch the water—the boiling water is too hot for the fragile custards usually cooked in a double boiler.

FRUIT DESSERTS

....

ah, the eternal question: chinos or jeans? And the other eternal question: is fruit a dessert? Well, if it wasn't before, it is now . . . But good fruit doesn't require much fussing with—simple preparations let the natural flavor reign.

Peaches, Blueberries, and Almonds en Papillote

Serves 4

baking these peaches and berries in parchment-paper pouches locks in all the juices. Which means the pouch is like a prison for flavor. A maximum-security prison. Aluminum foil can be substituted for the parchment paper.

Substitutions work well here: nectarines, blackberries, cherries, etc. Beware the usually horrible supermarket peaches and nectarines. Seek out only the best in-season fruit. The pouches need to be served hot from the oven, but the parchment paper packets can be prepared ahead of time and kept refrigerated for a couple of hours. One nice way to serve them is to snip open the tops with scissors and then allow each person to fold back the paper to reveal the fruit. Serve the pouches unadorned, or with a scoop of ice cream plopped right on top of the hot fruit. Sometimes I sprinkle mint leaves on the hot fruit.

4 ripe medium peaches
$1/2$ cup blueberries (fresh or frozen)
$1/4$ cup slivered almonds
1 tablespoon plus 1 teaspoon fresh lemon juice
$1/4$ cup sugar
2 tablespoons packed light brown sugar
2 tablespoons unsalted butter, cut into 4 equal pieces
12 mint leaves, optional

Preheat your oven to 400°F. Cut four 9 × 13-inch rectangles of parchment paper (or aluminum foil).

To peel the peaches, drop them into a pot of boiling water. Remove them after 20 seconds and plunge them into a bowl of ice-cold water. Slip the skins off, remove the pits, and slice the peaches into ¼-inch wedges.

In a bowl, combine the peaches, blueberries, almonds, and lemon juice. Add the granulated sugar and brown sugar and toss to combine.

To assemble the pockets, fold each parchment rectangle in half long-ways and crease it along the fold: this will help guide you. Open the paper and place one-quarter of the peach mixture just to one side of the crease. Add 1 piece of butter. Fold the other half of the paper over and then fold the three open sides tightly shut by creasing and crimping them.

Arrange the parchment pockets on a baking sheet and bake for 20 to 25 minutes, until they are puffed up and fragrant. Serve immediately. If you wish to add the mint, cut it into a fine chiffonade (slivers) and sprinkle it over the steaming-hot fruit.

Earl Grey Applesauce

Makes about 2½ cups

his isn't the pale, watery applesauce of your childhood, but rather a spicy, plummy, and very adult applesauce. While it's best made with fresh local apples, it will even work well with supermarket Golden Delicious apples that have been in cold storage for eight months. It's satisfying served alone, or with a dollop of whipped cream or cinnamon ice cream, but it's also great served atop or alongside cakes. Spoon it over Jam-Crowned Cupcakes (page 62). For breakfast, spread it on buttered toast, bagels, or biscuits. Feel free to double or triple the recipe. It keeps well in the refrigerator for about two weeks.

> 1 Earl Grey tea bag
> 1½ pounds apples (about 4 medium apples)
> ½ vanilla bean
> 8 prunes, pitted and chopped
> Pinch of grated lemon zest
> ⅓ cup sugar
> Pinch of ground cloves
> Fresh lemon juice to taste, optional

Pour ⅓ cup boiling water over the tea bag in a small cup and let it steep for 10 minutes. Meanwhile, peel and core the apples, and cut into wedges.

Combine the apples and the tea in a medium saucepan, discarding the bag. Split the vanilla bean and scrape the tiny seeds into the pan. Add the bean pod. Cover the pan and simmer for 10 minutes, stirring a few times.

Add the prunes and lemon zest and cook at a modest simmer for another 10 to 20 minutes, stirring occasionally. Remove the apple mixture from the heat when they are starting to break up and are soft enough to be mashed.

Remove the vanilla bean. Mash the apples with a potato masher to whatever consistency you prefer. Stir in the sugar, cloves, and lemon juice, if desired, stirring until the sugar is dissolved.

Serve at any temperature.

Berry Brûlée

Serves 4

this comforting and just-sweet-enough gratin is the epitome of simplicity—the perfect vehicle for fresh berries. You can feature one kind of berry or mix two or more together. You can bake the berries in individual ovenproof dishes—such as custard cups or crème brûlée dishes (my favorite)—or in a bigger gratin dish or pie plate. Just be sure the berries are in a thin layer—an inch or less.

> **2 cups (about 1 pint) fresh or frozen berries (see Note), washed, blotted dry, hulled if necessary, and large berries (such as strawberries) halved or quartered**
> **4 or more teaspoons packed light brown sugar**
> **A few dashes of framboise or other appropriate liqueur, optional**
> **Slivered almonds, pine nuts, or other nuts, optional**
> **¼ cup mascarpone cheese, cream cheese, or Neufchâtel cheese**

Position an oven rack about 4 inches from the broiler. Preheat the broiler.

Fill your ovenproof dish or dishes with the berries, making sure they're layered only about ½ to 1 inch deep. Sprinkle the berries with a little bit of the brown sugar. Add the framboise and toss in the nuts, if desired.

Dot the berries with dabs of the cheese. I like to cut the cheese with a knife so that it forms nice little slabs to lay on top—this way there is more surface area for the brown sugar to caramelize on. Mound the remaining brown sugar onto the cheese. If you're using individual dishes, place them on a sturdy baking sheet for easier handling.

Broil the brûlées for 4 to 6 minutes, until the brown sugar has caramelized and the berries are hot and just starting to show their juices. Watch the brûlées carefully lest they burn.

Serve immediately.

Note: Frozen berries will work, but it's best if they're about halfway thawed. Any less, and they won't heat up fast enough to release their flavor; any more, and they may be too mushy to handle (or recognize). Be sure to reserve any juices that are released as the berries thaw. Add the juices to the baking dish or dishes.

Slow-Roasted Pineapple Sauce

Makes about 1½ cups

most of the time, as those women who have dated me will confirm, I'm a bit of a dullard, a bit of a dud, a bit uninspired. But sometimes, if I do say so myself, I am a genius. Case in point: slow-roasted pineapple sauce. This easy and exquisite concoction isn't so much a dessert per se—it's too intense to be eaten alone. No, this thick sauce swimming with bits of pineapple isn't a dessert: it's what I like to call a dessert *catalyst*. It needs a venue before it can shine. Swirl it into good vanilla yogurt and you'll see what I mean. Or spoon it—still warm—over premium vanilla ice cream. It also goes well with cake. Try it with whipped cream on waffles too. Best fresh, it does keep well in the refrigerator. Still, a tiny dab of this dark, gooey concoction goes a long, long way—so feel free to halve the recipe.

1 medium pineapple
Grated zest and juice of 1 orange
7 ounces piloncillo (see Note), coarsely crushed, or 1
   cup packed dark brown sugar
¼ cup brandy
¼ cup heavy cream

Preheat your oven to 275°F.

Slice the top and bottom off the pineapple, then slice off the skin in strips. Remove the "eyes" with the tip of a paring knife or potato peeler. Cut the pineapple in half by slicing right down through the core. Now you can cut out the fibrous core by cutting out a wedge. Slice the pineapple into ¼-inch half-circles, and cut these into small tidbits.

Toss the pineapple, orange zest, and orange juice in a large glass baking dish. Sprinkle on the piloncillo, brandy, and cream.

Bake the pineapple for about 3 hours, stirring occasionally, until there are only a few tablespoons of juice left. The juice should be bubbly and slightly thickened, and caramelized. It will thicken further as it cools. Overcooking results in jamminess; undercooking, wateriness.

Serve the sauce warm. Or refrigerate and warm to at least room temperature before serving.

Note: Piloncillo is a traditional Mexican sugar made from cane juice that is boiled down and poured into cone-shaped molds. It has an earthy, dusky flavor that is particularly well matched to pineapple. Before you use it, you must wrap it in a towel and crush it with a hammer. You can find the cone-shaped plugs of piloncillo in Latin American markets or, increasingly, mainstream supermarkets. Dark brown sugar is a suitable substitute.

Slow-Roasted Orange Sauce

In place of the pineapple, use 12 medium oranges. First zest one of the oranges. Then you need to cut away all the peel and membranes from the orange segments. To do this, first slice off the top and bottom of each orange with a sharp paring knife. Then stand the orange on a cutting surface and cut the peel away in strips. If there's a lot of pith still on the orange, trim it off, but a little left on won't hurt. Now cup the "naked" orange in your palm—holding it over the baking dish to catch the juices—and cut carefully toward the middle of the orange on either side of each segment to free it from the membranes. The clean orange segments should come out easily. Remove any seeds as you go. When all the segments are free, squeeze any remaining juice from the pulp on the membranes, letting it drip into the dish.

The rest of the recipe is unchanged, except that you can omit the "juice of 1 orange," since the juice you squeeze from the membranes makes up for this.

Baked Pears with Pine Nuts, Dried Cherries, and Golden Raisins

Serves 4

a good baked pear is without equal—and this stuffed baked pear is my favorite. Bosc pears with their mottled brown skin and not-so-sweet flesh are my first choice for baking, but the more common Bartlett and d'Anjou pears work well, too.

4 ripe pears
¼ cup pine nuts
¼ cup dried cherries
¼ cup golden raisins
4 tablespoons (½ stick) unsalted butter, melted
¼ cup plus 2 tablespoons packed light brown sugar

Preheat your oven to 375°F. Butter the bottom of a baking dish large enough to hold the pears in a single layer, or spray it with nonstick cooking spray.

Wash the pears and halve them. With a melon baller or spoon, scoop out and discard their cores. Take a couple of more scoops out of each pear half, making a shallow hollow, being careful not to pierce the skin. Chop the scoops of pear, and put them in a mixing bowl.

Add the pine nuts, dried cherries, and golden raisins to the chopped pears. Stir. In a small bowl, stir the butter and brown sugar into a paste, then stir it into the dried fruit mixture until everything is thoroughly combined. Spoon this mixture into the pear halves and arrange the pears in the prepared baking dish.

Bake the pears for 25 to 35 minutes, until they are very soft when pierced with a sharp knife. Serve immediately.

Pineapple and Kumquat Salad

Serves 6

S ometimes dessert needs to be simple, particularly at the end of a rich or spicy meal. Fresh pineapple and kumquats are a natural pairing, and nothing could be prettier, especially in the winter. Unlike most citrus fruit, the peel of the kumquat is sweet and enjoyable.

1 ripe pineapple
5 to 20 kumquats

Peel and core the pineapple (see instructions with Slow-Roasted Pineapple Sauce, page 24). Cut it into slices, then into bite-sized bits. Put the bits and any juices in an attractive serving bowl.

Wash and dry the kumquats. Slice off and discard the ends. Slice each kumquat into thin rounds, discarding any noticeable seeds.

Scatter the kumquat slices over the pineapple, and serve. Or refrigerate for up to 24 hours before serving.

Banana Smoothies

Serves 2

I've mucked around with these smoothies ad nauseam but each time, I come back to the four-ingredient classic. It's smooth, nicely-flavored, refreshing, and easy to make. It's also my favorite way to use bananas that are slightly too ripe to be eaten otherwise. Never throw away an overripe banana again: just slice it, freeze the slices in a single layer on a cookie sheet (it takes at least one hour), and then make these smoothies. Or bag the frozen banana slices; they'll keep frozen for a week. This is a scaled-down recipe, but feel free to double or triple it, and blend it in batches. Add berries or chocolate syrup if you like. If you have an immersion blender, you can make these smoothies right in the serving glasses.

> 1 cup frozen overripe banana slices (about 1 medium
>   banana; see headnote)
> 1 cup milk
> 2 tablespoons sugar
> ½ teaspoon pure vanilla extract

Combine all the ingredients in a blender and process for 5 to 10 seconds. Serve immediately.

CUSTARDS

....

t's an old story, but a good one. Egg meets cream. Egg marries cream. Deliciousness, smoothness, and decadence ensue. Plus a little bit of jiggling.

Star Anise Pudding

Serves 8

W hen I first tasted these, I couldn't believe the flavor—straightforward, bold, and glorious. Star anise—the fruit of an evergreen tree—is indeed shaped like a star about as big as a quarter. It has a wonderfully warm and luxurious licorice flavor. Even though I had tasted all kinds of anise-flavored desserts and all kinds of custards, I wasn't prepared for how marvelous the combination would be. Which makes me wonder, why aren't there anise custard tarts, anise ice cream, anise milkshakes? Use the leftover egg whites to make Whole Wheat Poppy Seed Cake (page 64), a good angel's food cake, or meringue cookies. Egg whites can also be refrigerated for 2 days or frozen for 3 months.

10 star anise
2 cups heavy cream
1 cup milk
1 cup sugar
6 large egg yolks
1 teaspoon pure vanilla extract
Pinch of salt

Put the star anise in a plastic bag (or fold up in a clean towel) and crush thoroughly with a rolling pin. Combine the crushed anise, cream, milk, and sugar in a medium saucepan. Bring to a simmer over medium-high heat, stirring just until the sugar is dissolved. Remove the pan from the heat, cover it, and let the mixture steep for 45 minutes.

When the mixture has steeped, preheat your oven to 300°F.

Briefly whisk the egg yolks in a bowl. Slowly add the warm cream-anise mixture, whisking gently. Stir in the vanilla and salt.

Strain the custard through a fine-mesh strainer, then divide it among eight 4-ounce ramekins or custard cups.

Set the cups in a casserole dish and fill the dish with hot tap water to reach halfway up the sides of the cups. Bake the puddings for 55 to 65 minutes, until they are softly set but still a bit jiggly in the center.

Remove the puddings from the water bath and let them cool. Then cover the puddings and chill them for several hours, or overnight, before serving.

Raspberry Clafouti

Serves 8

Clafouti is a simple rustic dessert traditionally prepared with cherries. I happen to think that raspberries are better.
There's so much to love about this clafouti: it's not too sweet, it's basically foolproof, it's gorgeous, and it's unique. Fresh berries work best here, but frozen berries make a mean clafouti, too. If you're lucky enough to get golden raspberries, try them in combination with red berries for a real treat.

3 cups (about 12 ounces) fresh or frozen raspberries
½ vanilla bean
¾ cup milk
¾ cup heavy cream
3 large eggs
½ cup sugar
½ cup all-purpose flour
⅛ teaspoon salt
1 tablespoon framboise
Confectioners' sugar, for dusting

Preheat your oven to 375°F. Butter a 9-inch deep-dish pie pan and coat it with granulated sugar, knocking out any excess. Scatter the berries in the pan.

Split the vanilla bean and scrape the seeds into a saucepan; add the bean pod too. Add the milk and cream and heat over medium-high heat until small bubbles begin to rise. Remove from the heat. With an electric mixer, beat the eggs in a medium bowl while slowly adding the sugar. Then beat this mixture until thick and pale, about 2 minutes. Sift the flour and salt together and add them to the egg mixture in four stages, beating on low speed, mixing well after each addition.

Remove the vanilla bean from the milk mixture and slowly drizzle the milk mixture into the egg and flour mixture, beating at low speed. Finally, stir in the framboise. Pour the custard into the pie pan.

Bake the clafouti in the middle of the oven for 30 to 38 minutes, until puffy, browned, and set in the center. Dust with confectioners' sugar. Serve warm or at room temperature.

Three-Lemon Cheesecake

Serves 8

t he body of this easy cheesecake has a nice mellow lemony flavor, but it's the glaze that delivers the real zingy, zangy lemony punch. Serve it with whole berries or Raspberry Coulis (page 130).

CHEESECAKE
1 pound regular cream cheese
3 medium lemons, washed and dried
1/3 cup heavy cream
2/3 cup sugar
2 large eggs
1 tablespoon plus 1 teaspoon all-purpose flour

PIECRUST
1 cup graham cracker crumbs (7 or 8 whole crackers)
1 tablespoon sugar
Pinch of salt
2 tablespoons unsalted butter, melted

GLAZE
1/2 cup strained fresh lemon juice (from the 3 lemons)
1 1/2 tablespoons cornstarch
2 tablespoons sugar

First, remove the cream cheese from the refrigerator so that it can soften. It will be about the right temperature by the time it's needed.

Remove the zest from the lemons with a zester or grater. Reserve the lemons for later, leaving them out at room temperature, and put the zest in a small saucepan. Add the cream to the zest and heat just until the cream starts to bubble. Watch the pan carefully, since cream goes from bubbling to overflowing in a split second. Remove the pan from the heat, cover it, and let the zest steep for 45 minutes. In the meantime, prepare the cheesecake's crust.

Preheat your oven to 375°F.

Stir together the graham cracker crumbs, sugar, and salt. Stir in the butter until the mixture is uniformly moistened. With the bottom of a glass, press the crumbs into the bottom of a 9-inch springform pan. Bake the crust for 4 to 8 minutes, until it is barely browned at the edges. Let it cool.

When the zest/cream mixture has steeped for 45 minutes preheat your oven to 500°F.

Using a stand mixer or a powerful hand-held mixer, beat the cream cheese at low speed until smooth. Add the sugar and continue beating until smooth, scraping down the bowl regularly. Increase the speed to medium-high and add the eggs one at a time. Then beat in the flour. Finally, strain the lemon zest cream and add the cream, beating until the mixture is smooth and uniform.

Pour the batter into the prepared crust. Place the pan on a baking sheet to catch any leaks, and bake the cheesecake for 10 minutes. Lower the temperature to 200°F and bake the cheesecake for another 10 to 20 minutes, until it is light brown on top, cracked, and just barely set in the center.

Cool the cheesecake on a rack until it is slightly warm to the touch, then prepare the glaze.

Juice the reserved 3 lemons and strain the juice to remove any pulp and seeds. Measure out ½ cup of the juice (if you don't have ½ cup, add enough water to make ½ cup).

Put the cornstarch in a saucepan and whisk in the lemon juice. Heat the mixture over medium-high heat, whisking constantly, until it thickens to the consistency of pudding, 3 to 5 minutes. Remove from the heat and stir in the sugar. While the glaze is still hot, spread it evenly over the cooled cheesecake. Cover the cheesecake and chill it thoroughly before serving.

Queen of Puddings with Cherries

Serves 8

t his old, somewhat-neglected Southern favorite is a custardy bread pudding covered by a meringue made with the egg whites left over from the custard—a great idea. Traditionally, a thin layer of jam is spread between the custard and the meringue, but I think tart cherries add more interest, especially when paired with an orange-flavored custard.

CUSTARD
2 tablespoons sugar, plus more for the pie pan
½ vanilla bean
1 cup milk
1 cup heavy cream
3 large egg yolks
Grated zest of 1 orange
1½ cups fresh white bread crumbs

CHERRY SAUCE
2 tablespoons sugar
1 tablespoon cornstarch
Juice of 1 orange
2 cups frozen tart cherries

MERINGUE
3 large egg whites
⅓ cup sugar

Preheat your oven to 350°F. Grease a deep-dish 9-inch pie pan with vegetable shortening. Dump a couple of tablespoons of sugar in the pan and coat the pan with it, discarding any excess.

Split the vanilla bean. Scrape its tiny seeds out and add them to a saucepan, along with the pod. Add the milk and cream and heat over medium-high heat until small bubbles begin to rise. Remove the pan from the heat, cover, and let the mixture steep for 5 minutes.

Whisk together the egg yolks and sugar in a bowl, then whisk in the orange zest. Remove the vanilla bean from the milk/cream mixture and, whisking constantly, very slowly add the mixture to the egg yolks. Stir in the bread crumbs. Pour the mixture into the pie pan.

This custard needs to cook gently in a water bath, so find an ovenproof baking dish or roasting pan that is larger than the pie plate: a deep-dish pizza pan or broad skillet will work nicely. Center the pie pan in the empty pan, and add hot tap water to the larger pan until the water comes about halfway up the side of the pie pan and place both in the oven.

Bake the custard for 25 to 30 minutes, until it is softly set.

While the custard bakes, prepare the cherry sauce: Whisk together the sugar and cornstarch in a small saucepan, then whisk in the orange juice. Stir the mixture over medium heat until it becomes thick and puddinglike, 3 to 5 minutes. Add the cherries and stir occasionally until the cherries are thawed and the mixture is about room temperature. Set aside.

When the custard is done, remove it from the water bath, but leave the water bath in the oven. Prepare the meringue: beat the egg whites slowly in a large bowl until they begin to froth, then increase the speed to high and slowly add the sugar. Beat the whites until they form peaks that fold over just at the top.

Spread the cherry sauce gently over the cooked custard, then spread the meringue over the cherries. Return the pie pan to the water bath, replenish it if needed, and bake for about 15 minutes, or until the meringue is lightly browned. Let the pudding cool somewhat before serving.

Strawberry Crème Brûlée

Serves 8

....

trawberries and cream go together so perfectly, why not marry crème brûlée with strawberries? My favorite thing about this version is that the layer of strawberry cream—which starts at the bottom of the dish—floats to the top of the brûlée: Although it's a somewhat complex dessert to prepare, nearly all of the work can be done before company arrives. Other berries would work well in this recipe too, so feel free to experiment.

STRAWBERRY CREAM LAYER
1 pint strawberries (about 10 ounces), washed and hulled
½ cup heavy cream
2 tablespoons sugar
½ teaspoon fresh lemon juice, or more to taste

CUSTARD
3 cups heavy cream
½ cup sugar
Pinch of salt
1 vanilla bean
8 large egg yolks
About ⅓ cup turbinado or brown sugar, for topping

Puree the strawberries with the cream, sugar, and lemon juice in a food processor just until smooth. Don't overprocess the mixture, or the cream will turn into butter! Divide the mixture among 8 crème brûlée dishes or 5-ounce ramekins. Cover the ramekins and freeze until the mixture is solid, about 2 hours.

To make the custard, combine 1½ cups of the cream, the sugar, and salt in a saucepan. Split the vanilla bean and scrape its tiny seeds into the pan, then add the vanilla bean pod. Bring this mixture just to a boil over medium-high heat, stirring to dissolve the sugar. Remove the pan from the heat, cover it, and let it steep for 10 minutes.

Place a single layer of paper towels on the bottom of a baking dish or roasting pan big enough to contain all the crème brûlée dishes. Meanwhile preheat your oven to 300°F.

When the cream mixture has steeped, stir in the remaining 1½ cups cream. Whisk the egg yolks briefly in a medium bowl. Then very slowly add the warm cream mixture to the yolks, whisking gently but constantly. Strain the custard, and divide it among the crème brûlée dishes or ramekins.

Put the dishes in the prepared pan and place it in the oven, then very carefully pour enough hot tap water into the pan, being careful not to get any water in the crème brûlées, to come halfway up the sides of the dishes.

Bake the crème brûlées for 34 to 40 minutes, until they are softly set but still a bit jiggly. Don't be alarmed that the tops of the brûlées are now mostly pink. Remove the brûlées from the water bath and let them cool to room temperature.

Cover the brûlées tightly with plastic wrap and chill them for a minimum of 3 hours, or as long as 2 days.

About an hour before serving, position your oven rack 3 or 4 inches below your broiler element. Preheat your broiler. Sprinkle each brûlée with turbinado or brown sugar, tilting the dishes to spread the surface of each one with a thin, even layer of sugar. Knock out any excess sugar.

Put the brûlées on a sturdy baking sheet and broil the brûlées, moving or turning them occasionally if necessary to promote even broiling, until the sugar has melted and caramelized. Immediately remove the brûlées and chill them, uncovered, for 30 minutes before serving.

Rose Water Pots de Crème

Serves 6

hese diminutive, uber-silky custards are subtle and elegant, a fabulous way to end a meal with a series of ellipses instead of an exclamation point. Vanilla commonly flavors pots de crème, but rose water's floral tones are well suited to these not-too-sweet custards and certainly more unusual. Rose water, which before vanilla extract's widespread use was a common flavoring agent, is available in Middle Eastern food stores and from specialty baking supply stores, including The Baker's Catalogue (see Sources, page 137). Clean, fresh rose petals—untreated with pesticides—would be an appropriate garnish.

1 cup milk
⅔ cup heavy cream
4 large egg yolks
¼ cup sugar
½ teaspoon rose water

Preheat your oven to 325°F. Line a baking dish (one large enough to accommodate your six 4-ounce custard cups) or roasting pan with a kitchen towel or single layer of paper towels. Begin heating 5 to 6 quarts of water so that it will be boiling by the time you need it.

Combine the milk and cream in a saucepan and set it over high heat. Meanwhile, beat the egg yolks and sugar in a medium bowl for about a minute. When the milk and cream come to a boil (it will look more as if they are foaming than boiling), very gradually drizzle the mixture into the egg yolk mixture, whisking constantly but gently. Whisk in the rose water.

Strain the custard though a fine-mesh strainer. Divide it among six 4-ounce custard cups or ramekins, and arrange them in the towel-lined baking dish. Carefully add boiling water to the baking dish so that the water comes about halfway up the sides of the cups.

Bake for 22 to 28 minutes, until the custards are softly set but still quite jiggly in the center. Remove the custards from the water bath and let them cool. Then chill, covered, for at least 2 hours, or as long as 2 days, before serving.

PIES AND TARTS

....

Pies, as we all know, are the antidote to evil. Tarts, on the other hand, are the best example of perfection on earth. Even Plato admitted that. And galettes? Well, galettes are both.

Maple Custard Tart

Makes one 9-inch tart; serves 8 to 10

S imple, satisfying, and sublime—one of my new favorite desserts. Yet further evidence that the most basic desserts are often the best.

Easy Tart Dough (page 116), in a 9-inch fluted tart pan with a removable bottom, baked for only 10 minutes (see page 117) and cooled to room temperature

1 cup heavy cream

3 large egg yolks

⅓ cup pure maple syrup, plus more for garnishing

Preheat your oven to 350°F. Place the partially baked tart shell on a sturdy baking sheet.

Whisk the cream, egg yolks, and maple syrup until the mixture is uniform and smooth. Pour it into the tart shell. Bake the tart (on the baking sheet) for 22 to 28 minutes, until it is set.

Let the tart cool on a wire rack. Serve it at room temperature or chilled, with a drizzle of maple syrup.

Peach Pie with Almond Crumb Topping

Makes one 9-inch pie; serves 8

t he easy and scrumptious almond crumb topping reinvigo-
rates this classic pie's flavor and gives it a new look. Try
this topping on your favorite apple or berry pie, or sprinkle it
on some sugared apples or berries for a quick fruit crumble. If you
can't get good fresh peaches, substitute frozen peaches, which are
usually of decent quality.

**Shortening Piecrust (page 120) or Butter Piecrust
(page 122)**

FILLING
$^1\!/_2$ cup packed light brown sugar
$^1\!/_4$ cup sugar
2 tablespoons all-purpose flour
$^1\!/_4$ teaspoon cinnamon
$^1\!/_8$ teaspoon salt
6 ripe medium peaches or 5 cups frozen peach slices,
unthawed
2 teaspoons fresh lemon juice
1 teaspoon pure vanilla extract

TOPPING
$^1\!/_2$ cup blanched almonds (whole or pieces)
$^1\!/_4$ cup packed light brown sugar
$^1\!/_4$ cup plus 2 tablespoons all-purpose flour
6 tablespoons ($^3\!/_4$ stick) unsalted butter, cut into pieces

Roll out the crust, fit it into a 9-inch deep-dish pie pan (see
Note), and flute its edges. Cover it with plastic wrap and refrigerate while you prepare the filling.

For the filling, whisk together the brown sugar, granulated sugar, flour, cinnamon, and salt. Set aside.

To peel the peaches, drop them into boiling water for 20 seconds, then immediately transfer them to a large bowl of ice water. When the peaches have cooled, their skins should slip off easily.

Preheat your oven to 375°F.

Remove any stems from the peaches, pit them, and cut them into ¼-inch wedges. Toss them with the lemon juice and vanilla, then add the sugar mixture and toss well.

Spread the peaches in the pie shell, cover loosely with aluminum foil, and bake for 20 minutes.

While the pie bakes, prepare the topping: Process the almonds, brown sugar, and flour in a food processor until the mixture resembles coarse meal. Add the butter pieces and process until the mixture is uniform and there are no large pieces of butter left.

When the 20 minutes are up, carefully remove the hot pie from the oven and spread the crumb topping over the top, leaving about a 1-inch open border around the edge. Return the pie to the oven, without the aluminum foil, and bake for another 35 to 45 minutes, until the crust and topping are somewhat browned and the filling is bubbling at the edges. Frozen peaches may need additional baking time. (If you're using a glass pie pan, you can carefully lift up the pie to see how brown the bottom crust is.)

Cool the pie on a rack. Serve warm or at room temperature.

Note: If your pie pan isn't a deep-dish one, shape the crust to form a ¾-inch-high rim above the top of the pie pan, then flute the rim. This should hold all the filling.

Orange and Chocolate Chiffon Pie

Makes one 9-inch pie; serves 8 to 10

luffiness abounds. And a terrific flavor combination. With its Jell-O meets Cool Whip texture, the chiffon pie had its heyday decades ago, but its had a revival of late. It used to be made with uncooked eggs, but not anymore.

1 envelope unflavored gelatine
1 cup sugar
4 large egg yolks
2 tablespoons grated orange zest
½ cup fresh orange juice
¼ cup fresh lemon juice
2 ounces bittersweet chocolate, finely chopped
1 ounce unsweetened chocolate, finely chopped
1¼ cups heavy cream
Graham Cracker Crumb Piecrust (page 124), in a
   9-inch pie plate, chilled
Chocolate curls for garnish, optional

Sprinkle the gelatine over ¼ cup water in a medium saucepan and allow the gelatine to soften for 5 minutes.

Whisk ¾ cup of the sugar, the egg yolks, orange zest, orange juice, and lemon juice into the gelatine. Cook over medium heat, stirring constantly, until the mixture is steaming and slightly thickened, 8 to 12 minutes. Don't allow it to boil.

Strain the mixture into a bowl, then pour half the mixture back into the warm saucepan. Refrigerate the mixture in the bowl.

Sprinkle the bittersweet and unsweetened chocolates over the mixture left in the saucepan. Let stand for a few minutes to melt the chocolate, then gently whisk it in until smooth. Pour this mixture into a bowl and refrigerate it.

The idea now is to let your two gelatine mixtures cool down and just barely start to set. It should take somewhere around 30 minutes. Stir the mixtures frequently to see how set they are—once they start to set around the edges, they're probably ready. Remove them from the refrigerator and proceed.

Whip the cream with the remaining ¼ cup sugar until the cream forms soft peaks. Divide the whipped cream between the orange and chocolate mixtures. Beat the orange mixture (no need to clean the beaters) on low speed until smooth and uniform. Do the same with the chocolate mixture.

Spread the chocolate mixture over the piecrust, then carefully spread the orange mixture on top. Cover with an upside-down pie plate and chill the pie for at least 2 hours.

Garnish with curls of chocolate, if desired.

Black Walnut and
Dried Blueberry Tart

Makes one 9-inch tart; serves 8

I n the autumns when I was growing up, my sisters and I would sometimes spend a couple of afternoons picking up the black walnuts that fell from the trees on our farm. Then we'd take our load to the farmers' cooperative and they'd weigh the walnuts and pay us for them. If I recall, we usually got about a dollar and ten cents, which, split three ways, was simply demoralizing.

Part of the beauty of this tart is that it's a pantry tart—perfect for winter. I'm fond of the combination of black walnuts and dried blueberries, but there is an endless array of great substitutions possible here. Try pine nuts with currants or pecans with dried cherries, or experiment on your own. If you can't find black walnuts locally, try American Spoon Foods or The Baker's Catalogue (see Sources, page 137).

Serve the tart warm, at room temperature, or cool, with vanilla ice cream, whipped cream (page 129), or Crème Anglaise (page 127). My favorite way to eat leftovers is with a big glass of milk.

⅓ cup sugar
⅓ cup packed light brown sugar
¾ cup light corn syrup
2 tablespoons unsalted butter
2 large eggs
½ teaspoon pure vanilla extract
Pinch of salt
¾ cup chopped black walnuts (or other nuts)
⅓ cup dried blueberries (or other dried fruits or berries)
Easy Tart Dough (page 116), in a 9-inch fluted tart pan
    with a removable bottom, chilled

Preheat your oven to 350°F.

Bring the sugars and corn syrup to a boil in a saucepan. Remove the pan from the heat, add the butter, and stir until it is melted.

Beat the eggs briefly in a bowl, then slowly drizzle in the sugar mixture, whisking constantly. Whisk in the vanilla and salt. Stir in the walnuts and dried blueberries. Pour the mixture into the prepared tart crust.

Bake the tart for 25 to 35 minutes, until it is set and both the filling and crust are nicely browned. Allow it to cool on a rack before serving.

Hanging-Crust Rhubarb Cobbler

Makes one 8-inch square cobbler; serves 8 to 10

t he first rhubarb of spring is one of the season's best treats, and its ever-agreeable tartness suits the rich pastry crust of this Ozark cobbler, made in the manner of my mother and grandmother. Really, it's just a deep-dish pie, except that the ragged edges of the crust are folded over the filling—thus the "hanging" crust. Serve the cobbler warm, about an hour after removing it from the oven, with vanilla ice cream.

Note that this crust is designed to be very rich and tender, which, unfortunately, makes it somewhat delicate and difficult to handle. Don't fret, though: just patch it if it tears, and, by all means, don't worry about cosmetics.

FILLING
1¾ cups sugar
½ cup all-purpose flour
6 cups (about 2 pounds) rhubarb, cut into ¾-inch bits

CRUST
2 cups all-purpose flour
¾ teaspoon salt
¾ cup vegetable shortening
5 tablespoons ice water, more or less
Sugar for sprinkling, optional

Preheat your oven to 425°F.

To prepare the filling, combine the sugar and flour in a large bowl. Add the rhubarb and toss well. Set aside.

For the crust, combine the flour and salt. Cut in the shortening with a pastry cutter until the largest remaining bits of shortening are about pea-sized. Slowly sprinkle the water over the mixture while stirring with a fork just until the dough is moistened and clumps together. It should hold together when pressed.

Pat the dough into a flat square. Roll it out on a floured work surface (or lightly floured piece of wax paper) until not only is it large enough to come all the way up the sides of an 8-inch square glass baking dish, but there's even a bit more dough than necessary so that the edges can be folded over the top of the cobbler.

Carefully fit the crust into the baking dish. Add the rhubarb, spreading it evenly, then fold the edges of the crust over the rhubarb. There may be a bit too much crust in the corners when you fold them but you can remove a bit of the dough here and there and put it right on top of the filling, along with any other dough scraps.

If you wish for a nice crunchy-sugary top crust, brush the top crust with water and sprinkle it with sugar.

Bake for 50 to 55 minutes, until the crust is nicely browned and the filling is bubbly. Cool the cobbler on a rack.

Hanging-Crust Blueberry-Blackberry Cobbler

Substitute 4 cups fresh or frozen blueberries and 2 cups fresh or frozen blackberries for the rhubarb. Reduce the sugar to 1⅓ cups, and add ¾ teaspoon cinnamon and a pinch of salt to the flour-sugar mixture. Sprinkle 2 teaspoons fresh lemon juice over the berries and toss them briefly, then toss with the sugar-flour mixture.

Grapefruit-Lime Tart with Honey Poppy Seed Whipped Cream

Makes one 9-inch tart; serves 8

his canary yellow tart isn't bitter, and it won't squirt juice into your eye like a real grapefruit, but it does pack an intense citrus flavor, which the whipped cream tempers perfectly. I called earlier versions of this recipe "the tartest tart," but I toned it down a bit so that more people could enjoy it.

6 large egg yolks
½ cup sugar
Pinch of salt
½ cup freshly squeezed pink or Ruby Red grapefruit juice (from 1 grapefruit)
1 tablespoon plus 1 teaspoon fresh lime juice
8 tablespoons (1 stick) unsalted butter, cut into small pieces
Easy Tart Dough (page 116), in a 9-inch fluted tart pan with a removable bottom, prebaked (see page 117) and cooled completely

WHIPPED CREAM
1 cup heavy cream, chilled
1 tablespoon plus 1 teaspoon honey
1 tablespoon plus 1 teaspoon poppy seeds

Off the heat, whisk the eggs yolks in the top of the double boiler or a metal bowl until they are frothy, then whisk in the sugar, salt, grapefruit juice, and lime juice. Add the butter.

Place the top of the double boiler or the metal bowl over simmering water and stir the grapefruit-lime curd constantly. When the curd is steaming and has thickened to the point where it coats the back of your spoon thickly, it's done—this will take from 7 to 11 minutes.

Strain the thickened curd through a fine-mesh strainer into a waiting bowl. Put a piece of plastic wrap flush against the surface of the curd, so that a skin doesn't form, and allow it to cool for a while at room temperature. Then move it to the refrigerator and chill it for 3 hours, or overnight. (You can prepare the tart shell now, if you haven't already.)

To assemble the tart, pour the chilled curd into the baked tart shell and smooth it. Serve immediately, or return it to the refrigerator for up to 2 hours.

Just before serving, prepare the whipped cream: Whip all three ingredients in a chilled bowl with chilled beaters until the cream forms soft peaks.

Serve the tart with the whipped cream.

Apple Galette

Makes one 9-inch galette; serves 6

a galette is simply a free-form tart in a buttery crust. This apple galette is better than an apple pie—it's easier to make, and it's prettier than any pie I've ever seen. I use orange juice and zest to complement the flavor of the apples. Lemon juice, in my experience, only sharpens the flavor of apples.

Galette Dough (page 118), chilled

4 medium apples (1½ pounds or less)
½ cup sugar, plus more for sprinkling
1 tablespoon plus 1 teaspoon all-purpose flour
1 teaspoon grated orange zest
1 tablespoon plus 1 teaspoon fresh orange juice
¼ teaspoon cinnamon
Pinch of salt
2 tablespoons unsalted butter, cut into small pieces

If the chilled dough is too stiff to be rolled out, let it warm up at room temperature for a few minutes. Then, on a well-floured piece of parchment paper, roll the dough into a 14-inch circle. Don't worry about ragged or uneven edges—galettes are rustic tarts. Slide the parchment paper with the dough onto a baking sheet, cover the dough loosely with plastic wrap, and refrigerate while you prepare the apple filling.

Preheat your oven to 400°F.

Peel and core the apples. Cut them into very thin slices. Put all the apples in a microwave-proof dish with about 2 tablespoons water. Cover with plastic wrap and microwave until the apples are steaming and semi-soft, 2 to 5 minutes. Let the apples cool for a few minutes, then drain off and reserve any excess liquid.

Toss the warm apples in a bowl with all the other ingredients except the butter. Heap the apple slices in the middle of the rolled-out crust, leaving a 1½- to 2-inch border: do this by hand or with a spoon, so that you leave behind any liquid at the bottom of the bowl; set the bowl aside. Don't press down on the apples, or the bottom crust will become tough. Then dot them with the pieces of butter. Now gently fold the edges of the crust up over the apple pile, making pleats as you go. Handle the dough gently and be careful not to tear it or leave any holes. Pour any reserved juice over the apples still visible in the center of the galette.

With a pastry brush, gently brush the crust with water, then sprinkle it generously with sugar. Bake the galette (on the baking sheet) for 40 to 45 minutes, until the crust is nicely browned. If the galette leaks a little, don't fret—that's just the way of the world. Serve warm.

Blackberry Oatmeal Pie

Makes one 9-inch pie; serves 8

t here's something so pleasing and unassuming about this easy and unique pie. It's a happy combination of several homey flavors. I like to eat it in my pajamas.

Shortening Piecrust (page 120) or Butter Piecrust (page 122)

2½ cups blackberries, fresh or frozen
⅓ cup plus ¼ cup packed light brown sugar
3 tablespoons unsalted butter, softened
½ teaspoon cinnamon
½ teaspoon ground cloves
¼ teaspoon salt
⅔ cup light corn syrup
2 large eggs
⅔ cup quick-cooking oats

Preheat your oven to 350°F.

Roll out the dough and fit it into a 9-inch pie pan. Crimp the edges. Spread the blackberries in the crust. Sprinkle the ¼ cup brown sugar over the berries.

Beat the butter and the ⅓ cup brown sugar in a medium bowl until they clump together in a mass. Beat in the cinnamon, cloves, and salt. Beat in the corn syrup. Beat in the eggs one at a time. Stir in the oats. Pour the mixture into the piecrust.

Bake the pie for 55 to 65 minutes, until the crust is browned. Cool on a wire rack. Serve warm or at room temperature.

CAKES

· · · · · · · · · · · · · · · · · · · ·

What the visionary Marie Antoinette actually said was, "Let them eat *cakes*." Plural. She then went on to say, "Also let them enjoy tortes, cupcakes, little molten-centered chocolate cakes baked in individual ramekins, and those soft cakey things the British call 'pudding.' "

Chocolate Sinkholes

Serves 6 to 8

this is hands-down my favorite geologically titled dessert, better than the famous Landslide Mud Puppy and even the highly touted (but often poorly executed) Tectonic Tea Cake with Fruity Fissures. These rather refined-looking and super-chocolatey little cakes are baked in individual custard cups. The pretty crisp top of each cake collapses under gentle pressure, revealing the molten chocolate batter inside. Serve these cakes warm, with one perfect scoop of chocolate chip or vanilla ice cream in each sinkhole. Because this dessert is so intense, I give you two portion sizes—small and smaller. Believe me, even smaller is enough. . . .

8 tablespoons (1 stick) unsalted butter, cut into pieces
6 ounces bittersweet chocolate, chopped
¾ cup plus 2 tablespoons sugar
½ cup all-purpose flour
¾ teaspoon baking powder
⅛ teaspoon salt
4 large eggs
1 teaspoon pure vanilla extract

Melt the butter and chocolate in a double boiler or a metal bowl set over simmering water, stirring occasionally. Allow the mixture to cool to room temperature.

Preheat your oven to 325°F.

Sift the sugar, flour, baking powder, and salt together and set aside. Beat the eggs and vanilla in a medium bowl until frothy. Stir in the chocolate mixture until incorporated. Then slowly stir in the sugar-flour mixture just until everything is combined.

Divide the batter among six 6-ounce or eight 5-ounce custard cups or ramekins. Arrange the custard cups in a baking dish or roasting pan and fill the dish with enough cool tap water to come one-third of the way up the sides of the cups. (This water bath assures that the bottom portions of the cakes remain in a batter state.)

Bake for 34 to 38 minutes, until the tops are firm. Serve warm.

Jam-Crowned Cupcakes

Makes 12 cupcakes

t he thing about these rich and substantial cupcakes is that you don't have to fuss around with frosting. All you have to do is get out your favorite jam and spread some on top of the warm cupcakes. How easy is that? It's way too easy. It's also pretty. I like to use three or four different kinds of jam, so that there are many colors and flavors represented. And the hint of maple syrup in these cupcakes sets them apart.

12 tablespoons (1½ sticks) unsalted butter, cut into pieces, softened
¾ cup sugar
2 tablespoons plus 1 teaspoon pure maple syrup
1 teaspoon pure vanilla extract
2 large eggs
1½ cups all-purpose flour
1 teaspoon baking powder
¼ teaspoon salt
Jam(s) of your choice

Preheat your oven to 325°F. Line 12 standard-sized muffin cups with paper liners.

Beat the butter in a medium bowl until smooth. Add the sugar and continue beating until the mixture is pale, light, and fluffy: this could take several minutes, and is the most important part of the recipe.

Beat in the maple syrup and vanilla until incorporated. Then beat in the eggs one at a time, just until they are incorporated.

Sift together the flour, baking powder, and salt. Patiently fold this mixture into the butter mixture just until combined. Spoon the batter into the paper liners.

Bake the cupcakes for 18 to 24 minutes, until a cake tester or toothpick inserted in a cupcake comes out clean. Cool the cupcakes in the pan for a few minutes, then remove them and set them on a cooling rack.

While the cupcakes are still warm, spread the jam on their crowns. To do this most efficiently, stir the jam until it is smooth, then use the back of a spoon to spread a dollop onto each cupcake. You can spread the jam as thick or thin as you wish. I like to spread it relatively thin so that it is translucent and beautiful, almost like a lacquer on top of the cupcakes.

Snickerdoodle Cupcakes

That unmistakable snickerdoodle flavor is in these cupcakes, with their cinnamon-sprinkled crowns.

Make the cupcakes as directed above, but increase the vanilla to 1½ teaspoons and omit the maple syrup. Omit the baking powder, add 1 teaspoon cream of tartar, and increase the baking soda to ½ teaspoon. You can include ¼ teaspoon nutmeg, if desired, adding it with the flour. After the cupcakes have been in the oven for 10 minutes, sprinkle their crowns with a mixture of 2 tablespoons sugar and ¾ teaspoon cinnamon and continue baking.

Whole Wheat Poppy Seed Cake

Makes one 10-inch tube cake; serves 16

my mother developed this cake with a friend almost forty years ago, and despite my best efforts and cleverest tricks, I couldn't improve upon it. The whole wheat flour adds a rich and nutty background flavor that is perfect with the poppy seeds. The original recipe calls for maple flavoring, but vanilla extract works just as well. My favorite flavoring, though, is fiori di Sicilia, a combination of citrus oils and vanillin available from The Baker's Catalogue (see Sources, page 137). Plain citrus oils would be a great flavoring too, but don't use too much. This moist cake keeps well at room temperature or it can be frozen, and doesn't need any frosting. I always eat it plain, but it goes well with berries. Try to get your poppy seeds from a source that has a rapid turnover—they do go rancid pretty quickly.

2 cups whole wheat flour
1½ cups packed light brown sugar
1 tablespoon baking powder
1 teaspoon salt
½ cup canola oil
4 large eggs, separated, along with 3 or 4 additional
    egg whites to make 1 cup of whites
1½ teaspoons maple flavoring or pure vanilla extract or
    ½ teaspoon fiori di Sicilia
¾ cup poppy seeds
½ teaspoon cream of tartar

Preheat your oven to 350°F. Get out a 10-inch tube pan; do not grease it.

Sift together the flour, sugar, baking powder, and salt into a large bowl. Make a well in the center and add the oil, egg yolks, ¾ cup cold water, and the flavoring. Beat the batter until it is smooth. Stir in the poppy seeds.

Beat the egg whites with the cream of tartar in a large bowl until they form soft peaks. Pour the poppy seed batter over the whipped egg whites and gently fold the mixtures together just until barely combined. Don't overmix—there should still be streaks of egg whites visible.

Pour the mixture into the ungreased tube pan and bake for 45 to 60 minutes, until a cake tester inserted in the center comes out clean. Allow the cake to cool completely upside down before removing it from the pan.

Indispensable Chocolate Torte

Makes one 9-inch torte; serves 10

basic, beautiful and versatile. To my mind, it's the little black dress of the dessert world. Okay, that's a weird metaphor for a guy. Let's just say it can do anything, go anywhere. It includes only five ingredients, but it's so much more than the sum of its parts.

Here are some serving ideas:

- dust it with confectioners' sugar
- serve it with a modest dollop of Sweetened Whipped Cream (page 129)
- coat it with Jam Glaze (page 131)
- serve it with some vanilla yogurt and Slow-Roasted Pineapple Sauce (page 24)
- coat each plate with Crème Anglaise (page 127), place a piece of torte on the plate, then drizzle hot Caramel Sauce (page 126) over the torte
- soak it with a flavored syrup
- serve it with Raspberry Coulis (page 130) or Blackberry Coulis (page 130)
- serve it with crème fraîche and candied citrus peel
- coat it with Chocolate Ganache (page 132)
- sprinkle it with nuts
- serve it with ice cream, of course
- serve it with berries

5 ounces bittersweet chocolate, chopped
12 tablespoons (1½ sticks) unsalted butter, softened
⅔ cup sugar
5 large eggs, separated
½ cup all-purpose flour

Melt the chocolate in a double boiler or a metal bowl placed over simmering water, stirring occasionally. Remove from the heat and let cool until it's about body temperature.

Preheat your oven to 325°F. Grease and flour the sides of a 9-inch springform pan (see Note). Line the bottom of the pan with a round of parchment paper or wax paper.

Beat the butter until creamy. Then add ⅓ cup of the sugar and beat until smooth and fluffy. This could take several minutes. Beat in the egg yolks one at a time. Fold in the melted chocolate.

Beat the egg whites on low speed in a large bowl until they are foamy (like dishwater). Increase the speed to high and slowly add the remaining ⅓ cup sugar. Then beat until the egg whites form stiff peaks.

Stir one-quarter of the egg whites into the chocolate mixture, then gently fold in the rest of the egg whites until the mixture is uniform. Sift the flour onto the batter in 3 separate additions, folding it into the mixture after each addition.

Pour the batter into the prepared pan. Bake for 25 to 30 minutes, until the cake is somewhat spongy and a toothpick or cake tester inserted in the center comes out clean.

Let the torte cool in the pan on a rack. It will shrink, sink in the middle, and pull away from the sides of the pan. Serve warm or at room temperature.

Note: A sturdy 9 × 2-inch round cake pan can be substituted for the springform pan. Carefully slide a thin knife around the edges of the cake when it has cooled, then gently turn it upside down to remove it from the pan, then turn it right side up. The round of parchment paper or wax paper in the bottom of the pan should release the cake easily.

Hot Milk Sponge Cake
with Citrus Syrup

Makes one 9-inch square cake; serves 9

hen I tried out an old recipe for this unconventional sponge cake, I couldn't believe how easy and good it was. It's basically foolproof—no folding in of delicate egg whites or creaming of butter and sugar required. It's a fluffy, flavorful, versatile, and quick cake. You don't even have to grease the cake pan. And it's painfully low-fat, despite its great taste.

In addition to the citrus syrup and whipped cream frosting suggested here, the plain cake itself is a natural accompaniment for fresh berries or apricots. It will also accept almost any frosting. Or for something new, try the cider syrup.

1 cup cake flour or all-purpose flour
1 teaspoon baking powder
2 large eggs
¼ teaspoon salt
1 cup sugar
1 teaspoon pure vanilla extract
½ cup milk
1 tablespoon unsalted butter

CITRUS SYRUP
⅓ cup sugar
¼ cup strained fresh orange, lemon, lime, or tangerine
   juice (or any combination of these)

WHIPPED CREAM FROSTING
⅔ cup heavy cream
1 tablespoon sugar
1 teaspoon pure vanilla extract

Preheat your oven to 350°F. Line the bottom of a 9-inch square baking pan with parchment paper or wax paper.

Sift the cake flour and baking powder together, and set aside.

Beat the eggs and salt at high speed in a large bowl for 2 minutes. Continue beating for another 3 minutes while very slowly adding the sugar. The mixture will be thickened and foamy. Beat in the vanilla.

Bring the milk to a boil in the microwave (or in a saucepan). Add the butter to the hot milk and stir just until the butter melts. Add the hot milk to the whipped egg mixture, beating at medium speed until the mixture is uniform. Quickly add the sifted flour to the bowl and continue beating until the batter is smooth and there is no flour visible. Immediately pour the thin batter into the baking pan and put it in the oven.

Bake the cake for 18 to 24 minutes, until a toothpick or cake taster inserted in the middle comes out clean. Let the cake cool in the pan on a rack for 10 minutes. Run a thin knife around the edges of the cake and carefully turn the cake out of the pan onto a wire rack. Let the cake cool completely before applying the syrup and frosting.

Combine the sugar with ¾ cup water in a saucepan. Heat over medium-high heat, stirring occasionally, until the sugar dissolves. Off the heat, stir in the citrus juice.

To apply the syrup to the cake, place the cake on a serving plate and slowly pour the syrup over it.

For the frosting, beat the cream with the sugar and vanilla until it forms soft peaks. Spread it onto the cooled syrup-soaked cake. Serve it at room temperature or chilled.

CIDER SYRUP

I saw this syrup in Regan Daley's fantastic book *In the Sweet Kitchen*, and I knew it would pair perfectly with Hot Milk Sponge Cake. The fresher the cider, the better.

Boil 4 cups nonalcoholic apple cider until it thickens slightly and is reduced to about 1 cup. Pour over the cake while warm or at room temperature.

Peanut Butter and Chocolate Cake

Makes one 9-inch round cake; serves 8 to 10

easy, appealing, soft, and comforting—a cake reminiscent of childhood flavors, but not childish. It makes one round 9-inch cake, but you can double the recipe and stack the cakes on top of each other. You can also slice the single layer horizontally and put a layer of frosting or jam in the center for a peanut butter–jelly chocolate cake.

1 cup plus 2 tablespoons cake flour
¾ cup sugar
1½ teaspoons baking powder
½ teaspoon salt
½ cup milk
3 tablespoons smooth commercial peanut butter
2 tablespoons plus 1 teaspoon vegetable shortening
½ teaspoon pure vanilla extract
1 large egg

FROSTING
2 ounces unsweetened chocolate, chopped
4 tablespoons (½ stick) unsalted butter
1¾ cups plus 2 tablespoons confectioners' sugar
¼ cup milk
½ teaspoon pure vanilla extract
1/16 teaspoon salt

Preheat your oven to 350°F. Lightly grease and flour a 9-inch round cake pan and line the bottom with a round of parchment paper or wax paper.

Sift the cake flour, sugar, baking powder, and salt into a mixing bowl. Add the milk, peanut butter, vegetable shortening, and vanilla and beat for 2 minutes. Add the egg and beat for another 2 minutes.

Pour the batter into the prepared cake pan and bake for 26 to 32 minutes, just until a cake taster or toothpick inserted in the center comes out clean, or just barely moist.

Cool for 10 minutes in the pan on a rack, then run a knife around the edges of the cake and turn it out onto a rack to cool completely before frosting.

Melt the chocolate and butter in a double boiler or a metal bowl set over a pot of simmering water.

Slowly beat in the confectioners' sugar. When the mixture becomes a bit too thick to beat, add any remaining sugar and the milk, vanilla, and salt, beating until the frosting is smooth. Use the frosting immediately.

Sticky Toffee Pudding

Serves 6 or 9

m y parents came back from a visit to England and Scotland raving about sticky toffee pudding. This gooey-cakey wonder—drowned in caramel sauce—isn't seen much here, which is unfortunate. If you can get your hands on Medjool dates, by all means use them, but any dates—preferably organic—are fine.

4 ounces (about 1 cup) pitted dates, chopped
½ teaspoon baking soda
5 tablespoons unsalted butter, softened
¼ cup sugar
¼ cup packed light brown sugar
1 large egg
1½ cups all-purpose flour

CARAMEL SAUCE
1 cup packed light brown sugar
¾ cup heavy cream
3 tablespoons unsalted butter, cut into pieces

Preheat your oven to 350°F. Lightly grease 6 jumbo muffin cups with vegetable shortening. Alternatively, grease 9 standard muffin cups.

Combine the chopped dates and 1 cup water in a saucepan and bring to a boil. Remove from the heat and stir in the baking soda; the mixture will foam. Set aside.

With an electric mixer, cream the butter with both sugars in a medium bowl until the mixture is light and creamy; this will take several minutes. Beat in the egg. Stir in one-third of the date mixture (yes, include the liquid). Fold in half of the flour. Stir in another one-third of the date mixture, fold in the rest of the flour, and stir in the rest of the date mixture.

Divide the batter among the muffin cups. Bake for 20 to 24 minutes if using jumbo cups, 15 to 19 minutes if using standard-sized cups, until a cake tester or toothpick inserted in one comes out clean.

While the puddings bake, or as soon as they come out of the oven, prepare the caramel sauce: Combine all the ingredients in a saucepan and bring to a boil, stirring a few times. Pour about a third of the hot caramel over the puddings while they're still in the tins.

When it's time to serve the puddings, preferably while they're still warm, plate them (or, more appropriately, *bowl* them) and pour the remaining caramel sauce over them. Serve with a dollop of whipped cream or a scoop of vanilla ice cream.

Note: To prepare these cakes ahead of time, bake them as directed, then let them cool to room temperature—where they can remain for several hours, covered. Just before serving, plate the cakes and reheat them briefly in the microwave—just so they're warm. Then prepare the caramel sauce and pour it over the cakes.

COOKIES

....

hy cookies are the best desserts:

1. They can be eaten in one bite while no one is looking.
2. They fit in your pocket, even if it is sometimes a messy proposition.
3. They freeze well.
4. Breakfast on the go.
5. Lunch on the go.
6. Two words: "makes *dozens*."
7. Easy to double the recipe. Or triple.

Orange Drop Cookies

Makes about 50 cookies

hese soft and sublime cookies were one of my grandmother Jackson's most popular Christmas cookies, but I can't think of a reason why they shouldn't be enjoyed year-round. The sweet, tangy icing is the right topping for the pillowy cookies. These cookies freeze well.

¾ cup sugar
⅔ cup vegetable shortening
1 large egg
2 tablespoons finely grated orange zest
½ cup fresh orange juice (from 2 medium oranges)
2 cups all-purpose flour
½ teaspoon baking powder
½ teaspoon baking soda
½ teaspoon salt

ICING
2¼ cups confectioners' sugar
3 tablespoons plus 2 teaspoons unsalted butter,
    softened until nearly melted
1 tablespoon finely grated orange zest
2 tablespoons plus 1 teaspoon fresh orange juice
Pinch of salt

Preheat your oven to 400°F. Lightly grease two or three baking sheets with vegetable shortening or nonstick cooking spray, or line them with parchment paper.

Beat the sugar, shortening, and egg in a medium bowl until smooth. Beat in the orange zest and juice (you can strain the juice if you wish). At this point, the batter will look slightly curdled.

Sift together the flour, baking powder, baking soda and salt, then add to the batter, stirring until everything is incorporated.

Drop the dough onto the prepared baking sheets, 2 teaspoons per cookie, placed 2 inches apart. Bake for 6 to 9 minutes, just until the cookies are set and lightly browned on the bottom. Let the cookies cool briefly on the baking sheet before transferring them to a wire rack to cool.

When the cookies have cooled, prepare the icing by stirring all the ingredients together until smooth. Ice immediately.

Lemon Drop Cookies

In place of the orange juice in the dough, substitute ⅓ cup fresh lemon juice plus enough water to make ½ cup total; in place of the orange zest, use the zest of 1 lemon. In place of the orange juice in the icing, use 1 tablespoon plus 1 teaspoon lemon juice plus 1 tablespoon water; in place of the orange zest, use 2 teaspoons lemon zest.

Chocolate-Dipped Ranger Cookies

Makes about 50 cookies

t's true that I didn't invent ranger cookies. Or chocolate. But I did invent this combination of the two, which has a stellar cookie résumé: it's crispy-chewy, brown-sugary, and vanilla-y and has just the right amount of chocolate. And those little crescents of chocolate along the edges of the cookies are so gorgeous I want to eat them. Which is the whole idea.

1 cup all-purpose flour
$\frac{1}{2}$ teaspoon baking soda
$\frac{1}{4}$ teaspoon baking powder
Generous $\frac{1}{4}$ teaspoon salt
8 tablespoons (1 stick) unsalted butter, softened
$\frac{1}{2}$ cup vegetable shortening
$\frac{1}{2}$ cup plus 2 tablespoons packed light brown sugar
$\frac{1}{4}$ cup plus 2 tablespoons sugar
1 large egg
1 teaspoon pure vanilla extract
$1\frac{1}{4}$ cups old-fashioned oats
$\frac{3}{4}$ cup shredded sweetened coconut

CHOCOLATE DIP
$\frac{3}{4}$ cup semisweet chocolate chips
1 tablespoon vegetable shortening

Preheat your oven to 375°F. Grease two baking sheets with vegetable shortening or nonstick cooking spray, or line them with parchment paper.

Sift together the flour, baking soda, baking powder, and salt. Beat the butter and vegetable shortening in a medium bowl until combined and smooth. Beat in the brown sugar and granulated sugar, beating until the mixture is fluffy. Beat in the egg and vanilla until incorporated. Stir in the flour mixture. Stir in the oats and coconut until incorporated.

With greased hands, shape the dough into 2-teaspoon-sized balls and space them 3 inches apart on the baking sheets. Flatten the balls somewhat with your palm. Bake for 6 to 9 minutes, until the edges are modestly browned. Don't worry if the centers of the cookies look puffy and underbaked. Let the cookies cool for a few minutes on the sheets before transferring them to a wire cooling rack.

When the cookies are completely cool, you're ready to dip their edges in the chocolate.

For the chocolate dip, melt the chocolate chips and shortening together in the microwave or a small bowl over simmering water. Stir to combine. Dip the cooled cookies in the chocolate so that just one edge is covered with chocolate—it should make a thin crescent moon shape—and place the dipped cookies on wax paper- or parchment paper–covered baking sheets. Chill until the chocolate is set, about 20 minutes.

Cakey Rhubarb Bars

Makes a 9-inch square pan of cookies

these unique bar cookies are famous in my family because of their true name: Rhubarb Sauce. Sauce? What sauce? These are *cookies*, my friend, not sauce. Anyhoo, whatever they are, they're deadly and delicious. There's something perfect about the shortbread base paired with the rhubarb topping. These cookies are very cakelike. In fact, you can serve them as cake by plating them individually and serving them with a spoonful of sour cream or whipped cream (see page 129). However you enjoy them, keep in mind that they're best the day they're made.

CRUST
1 cup all-purpose flour
5 tablespoons confectioners' sugar
8 tablespoons (1 stick) unsalted butter, cold
¼ teaspoon salt

"SAUCE"
2 large eggs
¾ cup packed light brown sugar
¼ cup all-purpose flour
¾ teaspoon baking powder
¼ teaspoon salt
2 cups finely diced rhubarb (about ¾ pound, 3 to 4 stalks)

Preheat your oven to 350°F. Lightly grease a 9-inch square baking pan with vegetable shortening.

For the crust, combine all the ingredients in a bowl and cut them together with a pastry cutter until the mixture is crumbly and fine. Alternatively, cut the butter into pieces and pulse the ingredients together in a food processor until the same consistency is achieved. Spread the mixture into the greased pan and lightly pat it down. Bake the crust for 12 to 16 minutes, until it is slightly puffed and just barely showing hints of brown around the edges. Remove from the oven, and let cool on a rack.

Leave the oven at the same temperature while you make the "sauce."

Whisk the eggs well in a medium bowl—30 seconds or so—then stir in the brown sugar, flour, baking powder, and salt. Stir until the mixture is smooth, then stir in the rhubarb. Pour the mixture onto the baked bottom crust, spreading the rhubarb fairly evenly.

Bake for 26 to 32 minutes, until the topping is set and quite brown. It's easiest to remove the cookies if you let them cool thoroughly first before cutting them into bars.

Molasses Softies with Candied Ginger

Makes about 25 cookies

t hese spicy, soft, autumnal cookies are easy to make and inviting. What's not to love? Molasses cookies are a dime a dozen, but the candied ginger adds a vibrancy that makes these stand out.

8 tablespoons (1 stick) unsalted butter, softened
½ cup sugar, plus ¼ cup for coating the cookies
½ cup molasses (not blackstrap)
1 large egg
2 cups all-purpose flour
1 teaspoon cinnamon
½ teaspoon ground ginger
½ teaspoon salt
½ teaspoon baking soda
½ cup diced candied (a.k.a. crystallized) ginger

Preheat your oven to 350°F. Lightly grease two or three baking sheets with vegetable shortening or nonstick cooking spray, or line them with parchment paper.

With an electric mixer, cream the butter and sugar until the mixture is soft and fluffy, about 5 minutes. On low speed, beat in the molasses and egg just until the mixture is uniform.

Sift together the flour, cinnamon, ground ginger, salt, and baking soda. Stir into the batter. Stir in the diced candied ginger.

Put the ¼ cup sugar in a shallow bowl. Roll the cookie dough into balls about the size of golf balls, or slightly smaller. Roll the balls in the sugar to coat, then place them on the prepared baking sheets, 3 inches apart.

Bake for 12 to 16 minutes, until set and crackled. Let them cool briefly on the baking sheets before transferring them to racks to cool completely.

Mocha Mousse Wafers

Makes about 40 cookies

hese soft and silky little cookies don't contain a lick of flour. They're dark and intense and unlike any cookie you've ever had. But because they're delicate, they need to be served frozen. Otherwise, they might turn into goo. Yummy-tasting goo, but goo nonetheless.

4 tablespoons (½ stick) unsalted butter, cut into pieces
4 ounces bittersweet chocolate, chopped
2 teaspoons instant espresso powder, dissolved in 2
    teaspoons hot water
3 large eggs, separated
Pinch of salt
3 tablespoons packed light brown sugar, sifted

Preheat your oven to 325°F. Line two or three baking sheets with parchment paper. (There's no substitute for the parchment paper here, I'm afraid.)

Melt the butter and chocolate in the top of a double boiler or a metal bowl set over a pan of simmering water. Remove from the heat and whisk in the dissolved espresso. Let this mixture cool for several minutes, then whisk in the egg yolks.

Beat the egg whites with the salt in a medium bowl on low speed until they are frothy. Increase the speed to high and slowly add the brown sugar, beating until the whites form soft peaks.

Fold one-third of the beaten whites into the chocolate mixture to lighten it. Then gently fold in the rest of the whites. The batter should be light and fluffy—a mousse.

Drop the batter onto the parchment paper, about 1 tablespoon per cookie, spacing them about 2½ inches apart. Bake the cookies for 5 to 8 minutes, until they are puffed and not too glossy. Slide the parchment paper (with the cookies still on it) onto racks to cool.

Once the cookies have cooled, leaving them on the parchment paper, freeze them until they're firm enough to remove from the paper. Keep them frozen until serving.

Internal Jams

Makes about 30 cookies

had a dream, a simple dream, a pleasing dream—a dream of beautiful and enchanting sugar cookies that had jam inside them. A dream of cookies that would change the way we looked at the world, change the way we treat each other. Also, they would taste good. This was the dream of the internal jams. And through trial and error, via sweat and tears, with my friends butter and sugar by my side, I worked to make this dream a reality. I worked on weekends. I worked on national holidays. Sometimes I didn't even answer the phone. Or shower. And I ate a lot of so-so internal jams. Until finally, one day, I created a batch of cookies so perfect and so right that after I tasted one I simply nodded to myself, took a step backward in order to survey the gorgeous batch of still-warm cookies, and smiled—because it is rare for dreams to become real. . . .

My favorite jam for these is black raspberry.

½ pound (2 sticks) unsalted butter, softened
1 cup minus 1 tablespoon sugar
1 tablespoon packed light brown sugar
1 large egg
1 teaspoon pure vanilla extract
2 cups plus 2 tablespoons all-purpose flour
½ teaspoon baking powder
¼ teaspoon plus ⅛ teaspoon salt
Jam of your choice
Sanding sugar (or regular granulated sugar), for
    decoration

Beat the butter and sugars together in a large bowl until light and fluffy, 3 to 5 minutes. Beat in the egg and vanilla just until incorporated.

Sift together the flour, baking powder, and salt. Add to the batter and beat on low speed until incorporated. Cover the dough and refrigerate it until chilled, 1 hour or more.

Preheat your oven to 375°F. Line two baking sheets with parchment paper, or lightly grease them with vegetable shortening.

When the dough is chilled, pinch off a 1-tablespoon piece and roll it into a ball. Flatten the ball between your palms. Now shape it into a small bowl shape—like shaping a clay pinch pot. Drop ½ teaspoon of jam into the bowl and pinch the bowl shut. Gently flatten the cookie slightly, with the pinched seam on the bottom. Dip the smooth top of the cookie in a small bowl of the sanding sugar, then place the cookie on a prepared baking sheet. Repeat to make more cookies. Don't crowd the cookies on the sheet—while they don't spread much, they need plenty of room in order to cook evenly. I usually put 8 cookies on each baking sheet.

Bake the cookies one sheet at a time for 10 to 14 minutes, just until they are lightly browned at the edges and on their bottoms. Let the cookies cool for 3 minutes on the sheet before transferring them to a rack to cool completely.

Coconut-Lime Coolers

Makes about 40 cookies

hese are perfect little mouthfuls because of the zany flavor of the lime balanced against the coolness of the powdered sugar and the richness of the coconut.

¾ cup shredded sweetened coconut
2 teaspoons grated lime zest
1½ cups all-purpose flour
¼ teaspoon ginger
¼ teaspoon baking powder
¼ teaspoon salt
⅔ cup confectioners' sugar, plus about ⅓ cup for coating the cookies
8 tablespoons (1 stick) unsalted butter, softened
1 tablespoon canola oil
2 large egg yolks
1 tablespoon fresh lime juice
¼ teaspoon lemon extract

Preheat your oven to 325°F. Grease two baking sheets with vegetable shortening or nonstick cooking spray, or line them with parchment paper.

In a food processor, process the coconut and lime zest until fine. Sift together the flour, ginger, baking powder, and salt.

Beat the ⅔ cup confectioners' sugar, the butter, and oil in a medium bowl until very smooth. Beat in the egg yolks, lime juice, and lemon extract. On low speed, beat in the flour mixture until it comes together, then stir in the coconut and lime zest.

Form the dough into tablespoon-sized balls, place them 2 inches apart on the baking sheets, and bake for 15 to 20 minutes, until the bottoms are moderately browned. Let the cookies cool on the sheets for a few minutes before transferring them to a wire rack to cool. While the cookies are still warm, put the ⅓ cup confectioners' sugar in a small bowl and roll them in the sugar to coat.

FROZEN DESSERTS

···

the Roman emperor Nero used to send runners all the way
to the Alps to fetch snow to make ice cream with. Little did
he know that all he needed was some cream, eggs, sugar, flavoring, and a forty-dollar ice cream maker. But then, he *was* crazy.

Mint Leaf Ice Cream

Makes about 1 quart

no retina-damaging neon green dye, no chemical mint taste—this is the real thing, and it's probably unlike any ice cream you've ever tasted. The real mint adds a freshness and mellowness you can't get from mint extract. Serve with Blackberry Coulis (page 130) or room-temperature Rich Chocolate Sauce (page 125).

> **4 large egg yolks**
> **²/₃ cup sugar**
> **⅛ teaspoon salt**
> **1½ cups milk**
> **35 mint leaves**
> **1½ cups heavy cream**
> **¼ teaspoon pure vanilla extract**

Beat the egg yolks, sugar, and salt in the top of a double boiler or metal bowl until the mixture is pale yellow and slightly thickened. Set aside.

Heat the milk in a saucepan over medium-high heat until it just starts to bubble. Slowly drizzle the hot milk into the egg mixture, stirring steadily.

Heat this custard mixture over simmering water, stirring constantly, until it's a bit thicker than heavy cream, 7 to 10 minutes. Immediately pour it into a clean bowl and stir in the mint leaves. Then stir in the cream and vanilla. Allow the custard to cool to room temperature, then refrigerate it until well chilled, at least several hours or overnight.

Just before making the ice cream, strain out the mint leaves from the custard, pressing against the mint for more flavor, if desired. Freeze the ice cream according to your ice cream maker's directions. When the ice cream is done, you can serve it immediately if you want soft ice cream. For a thicker, more commercial-style ice cream, transfer the ice cream to a freezer container and freeze for at least 2 hours.

White Chocolate
and Nectarine Ice Cream

Makes about 1 quart

White chocolate alone is a flavor that tends to fade into the background, but nectarines not only complement it, they seem to make it bigger and brighter. All this makes for a unique ice cream.

   4 ounces white chocolate, chopped
   3 large egg yolks
   ½ cup sugar
   2 cups heavy cream
   ⅔ cup milk
   ½ pound ripe nectarines (about 2 good-sized
      nectarines) or peaches
   1 tablespoon fresh lemon juice
   ¼ teaspoon pure vanilla extract
   ⅛ teaspoon salt
   Chopped pistachios, for topping, optional

Start about an inch of water simmering in the bottom of a double boiler or a medium saucepan. Put the chopped chocolate in the top of the double boiler or a metal bowl, off the heat. Beat the egg yolks and sugar in a medium bowl until pale yellow and thick.

Meanwhile, heat the cream and milk in a saucepan to just below the boiling point—you'll see tiny bubbles rising to the surface. Pour about half of this hot mixture over the chocolate, whisking until the chocolate is melted. Drizzle the other half of the hot cream mixture into the thickened egg yolks, whisking constantly. Stir the egg yolk mixture into the chocolate mixture.

Heat the mixture over simmering water, stirring constantly, until thickened, 7 to 10 minutes. Let the custard cool to room temperature while you prepare the nectarines.

Over a bowl, grate the nectarines on a cheese grater. Discard the skins—they won't go through the grater. Stir the lemon juice, vanilla, and salt into the nectarine pulp.

Chill the nectarine mixture and the custard separately for several hours, or overnight.

Just before making the ice cream, combine the two mixtures. Freeze the ice cream in accordance with your ice cream maker's directions. For a soft ice cream, serve immediately. For a firmer, more commercial-style ice cream, transfer to a freezer container and freeze for at least 4 hours.

Sprinkle individual servings with chopped pistachios, if desired.

Ginger Sherbet

Makes about 1½ quarts

The icy, bracing taste of this sherbet is for true ginger lovers. The flavors shine through with remarkable clarity and vigor. If you're not comfortable using raw egg whites, leave them out; the texture will suffer only slightly.

½ vanilla bean
1 cup sugar
¼ cup finely chopped fresh ginger
⅛ teaspoon salt
3 cups milk
3 large egg whites

Split the vanilla bean and scrape the tiny seeds into a saucepan. Add the vanilla bean pod, as well as 1 cup water, the sugar, ginger, and salt. Bring to a boil, stirring occasionally, then reduce the heat and simmer for 5 minutes. Remove from the heat.

Meanwhile, heat the milk in a medium saucepan over medium-high heat just until small bubbles start to break the surface. Remove from the heat and stir in the ginger-sugar mixture. Cover and let steep for 45 minutes.

Strain the mixture, pressing against the ginger for more flavor, if desired. Chill the mixture for several hours, or overnight.

Just before making the sherbet, whip the egg whites to soft peaks. Gently fold them into the chilled mixture. Make sure the eggs whites are well incorporated—not just floating on top. Freeze the sherbet according to your ice cream maker's directions. For a soft sherbet, serve immediately. For a denser, more commercial-style sherbet, transfer to a freezer container and freeze for at least 3 hours.

Toasted Coconut Ice Cream

Makes about 1 quart

T he secret here is to use a fresh coconut—not preshredded packaged coconut that has been sitting in the supermarket for months. Using real coconut gives the ice cream a flavor and richness that is heavenly. I'm not saying that it's easy—processing a coconut is a lot of work—but it's worth the trouble.

1 coconut, with plenty of juice sloshing inside
½ vanilla bean
¾ cup milk
1 cup sugar
⅛ teaspoon salt
4 large egg yolks
1¾ cups heavy cream

Preheat the oven to 325°F.

Pierce two of the "eyes" of the coconut with a corkscrew or heavy skewer, being careful not to cut yourself. Drain out the juice and reserve.

Wrap the coconut in a kitchen towel and whack the heck out of it with a hammer on a hard surface, like a sidewalk. Crack the larger pieces into smaller pieces, then pry the coconut meat from the shell with a dull knife or screwdriver. Remove the brown skin with a vegetable peeler.

Rinse the coconut meat pieces, pat them dry, and then coarsely grate with a cheese grater or with the grater blade in a food processor. You only need 1 cup of grated coconut for this recipe, so you don't have to grate all the coconut. The extra coconut should keep for a few days in the refrigerator. Or you can go ahead and grate and toast all of the coconut. Toasted, it keeps well, and you can sprinkle it on the ice cream as a garnish, or add it to yogurt or breakfast cereal.

To toast the coconut, spread it *thinly* (use two baking sheets if you want to toast all the coconut) on a baking sheet and place it in the oven for 10 to 15 minutes, stirring occasionally, until the coconut is light golden. The time required to reach the perfect degree of toasting will depend on how much coconut you're trying to toast at once.

Now for the ice cream custard base: Split the vanilla bean and scrape its tiny seeds into a saucepan. Add the bean pod, as well as 1 cup of the toasted coconut, the milk, ¾ cup of the sugar, and the salt. Strain ½ cup of the white coconut juice you set aside earlier and add it to the pan. Heat the mixture, stirring occasionally, just until the first bubbles start to rise. Remove the pan from the heat, cover it, and allow to steep for 30 minutes.

Heat the mixture again, taking it off the heat just when it starts to bubble.

Meanwhile, whisk together the final ¼ cup sugar and the egg yolks in the top of a double boiler or a heatproof bowl until the mixture is slightly paler and thicker. Strain the coconut-milk mixture, then drizzle it into the egg-sugar mixture, whisking constantly.

Cook the mixture over simmering water, stirring constantly, for 7 to 10 minutes, until it is thicker than heavy cream. Remove from the heat and stir in the cream.

Chill the custard for several hours, or overnight.

Freeze the ice cream according to your ice cream maker's directions. For a soft ice cream, serve immediately. For a thicker, more commercial-style ice cream, transfer the ice cream to a freezer container and freeze for several hours.

Garnish with extra toasted coconut or chocolate shavings, if desired.

Fresh Snow Ice Cream
(a.k.a. Snice Cream)

Serves 6

When I was a kid, there was nothing quite as magical as snow ice cream, which we were lucky to get once a year. I was surprised to find that the novelty and uniqueness of this treat is still just as enjoyable now that I'm grown up. The ice cream melts instantly in your mouth. It's unlike any commercial ice cream. Just be sure your snow is clean and fresh—gathered the same day it falls.

⅔ cup heavy cream
1 to 2 tablespoons pure vanilla extract, to taste
1 cup confectioners' sugar
About 10 cups fresh, clean, fluffy snow

Before starting the recipe, put a large mixing bowl, your mixer's beaters, and individual serving bowls in the freezer for at least 20 minutes.

Beat the cream, vanilla, and confectioners' sugar together in the frozen mixing bowl just until the mixture is well thickened—not whipped and fluffy. Immediately fetch the snow from outside, dump it into the bowl, and quickly fold the mixture together. It will probably look clumpy, but that's okay. Overmixing or hesitating will result in slush.

Serve the ice cream immediately in the frozen bowls.

Black Grape Sorbet

Makes about 3½ cups

t he simplicity of this sorbet is its strength. The pure grape flavor is bright and refreshing, and the beautiful purple color of the sorbet couldn't be replicated by any artificial coloring.

1 cup sugar
1 pound (about 4 cups) seedless black grapes, washed
   and stemmed
2 tablespoons fresh lemon juice, or to taste

Heat the sugar with 2 cups water in a saucepan stirring occasionally, until the sugar is dissolved. Remove the syrup from the heat.

Combine the grapes and lemon juice in a food processor. Pour about half of the warm sugar syrup over the grapes, then puree them well.

Strain the mixture through a medium-mesh sieve, pressing against the grape pulp to extract as much liquid as possible. Stir in the rest of the sugar syrup. Cover and chill the mixture for at least a few hours or overnight.

Freeze the sorbet according to your ice cream maker's directions. For a slushy sorbet, serve immediately. For a firmer sorbet, transfer the sorbet to a freezer container and freeze for at least 2 hours.

If the sorbet freezes too firm to scoop, you can let it soften in the fridge for 20 or more minutes, or scoop it with a scooper that has been dipped in warm water.

Lemon Custard Ice Cream

Makes about 5 cups

unrepentantly rich. Supremely smooth. Lemony goodness. Soft and creamy and joyful in the mouth.

4 medium lemons, washed and dried
2⅔ cups heavy cream
6 large egg yolks
1 cup plus 1 tablespoon sugar
⅛ teaspoon salt

Zest the lemons with a zester or grater; reserve the lemons. Bring the cream and the zest to a simmer in a saucepan. Remove from the heat, cover, and allow to steep for 30 minutes.

Beat the egg yolks, sugar, and salt in the top of a double boiler or a heatproof bowl until the mixture is pale yellow.

Meanwhile, bring the cream mixture to a simmer again. Strain the cream mixture and slowly drizzle it into the yolk mixture, while whisking constantly.

Cook the custard over simmering water, stirring constantly, until it is nicely thickened, 8 to 12 minutes. Cover the custard and chill it for several hours, or overnight.

Just before making the ice cream, juice the lemons and strain the juice through a fine-mesh strainer. Stir ½ cup of the strained juice into the custard.

Freeze the ice cream according to your ice cream maker's directions. For a soft ice cream, serve immediately. For a firmer, more commercial-style ice cream, pack the ice cream in a freezer container and freeze for at least 3 hours.

Cup o' Pie/Pie in a Cup

Serves 1

Well, most of us like ice cream with our pie, so why not combine the two into a milkshake? Feel free to try any kind of pie—although there are some kinds of pie that I don't think would work, like lemon meringue or pecan pie. I like berry pies, but my favorite, without a doubt, is pumpkin pie.

This is more of a formula than a recipe, since each kind of pie will react in a slightly different way, so feel free to add a little more or less ice cream or milk. I sometimes let the ice cream sit in the blender for 10 minutes to soften before blending.

**A modest piece of pie (one-eighth of a 9-inch pie),
preferably at room temperature or cold
4 scoops vanilla ice cream
2 tablespoons milk**

Combine all ingredients in a blender and blend until the desired consistency is reached. Serve immediately.

UNCATEGORIZABLE DESSERTS

don't think of them as orphans or misfits. Think of them as so original they defy convention.

Eve's Pudding with Cinnamon and Anise

Serves 6

my trumped-up version of this British dessert is rich and satisfying and pretty. It's just a simple cake batter baked on top of sweetened apples in individual dishes. Plan to have it come out of the oven just before you sit down for dinner—it will be just the right temperature in time for dessert.

APPLE FILLING
4 small to medium baking apples, peeled, cored, and
   thinly sliced
1/2 cup sugar
1/4 cup packed light brown sugar
1/8 teaspoon salt
2 tablespoons plus 2 teaspoons fresh lemon juice
1 cup heavy cream
12 cinnamon sticks

CAKE TOP
1 1/3 cups all-purpose flour
2 teaspoons baking powder
2 teaspoons ground star anise
3/4 teaspoon salt
8 tablespoons (1 stick) unsalted butter, softened
2/3 cup sugar
2 large eggs

Preheat your oven to 325°F. Have six 10-ounce soufflé dishes ready.

Toss the apples slices with the granulated sugar, brown sugar, salt, and lemon juice. Set the mixture aside while you prepare the cake.

Sift together the flour, baking powder, anise, and salt. Stir to combine.

Beat the butter and sugar together in a medium bowl until fluffy. Beat in the eggs until the mixture is smooth. Stir in the flour mixture until thoroughly combined.

Divide the apple mixture among the soufflé dishes. Divide the cream among the dishes. Spread the cake batter over the top of the apples, spreading it so that the edges are sealed all around. Poke 2 cinnamon sticks into each pudding, leaving just a little bit of each stick protruding.

Bake the puddings directly on the oven rack for 35 to 45 minutes, until the cake is firm. Serve warm.

Hot Vanilla

Serves 4

We all love hot chocolate, so why not hot vanilla? The double vanilla flavor adds a more complex taste. Add a dash of nutmeg or cinnamon if you want.

4½ **cups milk**
3 **tablespoons sugar, plus more to taste**
1 **teaspoon pure vanilla extract**
1 **vanilla bean**

Combine the milk, sugar, and vanilla extract in a medium saucepan. With a paring knife, split the vanilla bean in half and scrape the tiny seeds into the milk. Add the vanilla bean pod and stir the mixture over medium heat just until small bubbles start to rise, about 5 minutes. Remove the mixture from the heat, cover, and let it steep for 30 minutes.

Taste for sweetness, and add more sugar if desired, then gently heat the milk back to serving temperature. Remove the vanilla bean and serve.

Apple-Pumpkin Bagel Pudding

Serves 8

day-old bagels are often too stale to eat, but they make great bread pudding. If you don't have stale bagels sitting around, many bagel stores sell their day-old bagels dirt cheap. This bread pudding is actually better for breakfast than for dessert, but maybe that's just my preference. Plain bagels work fine, but I really like to use poppy seed bagels. Dress it up with a drizzle of crème anglaise.

2 medium bagels (6 to 8 ounces total), preferably a
    day old
1¼ cups milk
¾ cup heavy cream
1 cup canned pumpkin
3 large eggs
½ cup sugar
½ cup packed light brown sugar
4 tablespoons (½ stick) unsalted butter, melted
1 teaspoon cinnamon
½ teaspoon nutmeg
¼ teaspoon salt
½ cup raisins
1 apple, peeled, cored, and diced
½ cup pecans, chopped

Preheat your oven to 350°F. Butter a 2-quart glass baking dish.

Cut 1 of the bagels into chunks and process it in a food processor to make fine crumbs. Cut the other bagel, by hand, into small pieces. Combine the bagels in a large bowl.

Heat the milk and cream in a saucepan over medium-high heat just until small bubbles start to rise. Pour the milk-cream mixture over the bagel crumbs and pieces, and set aside.

Whisk together the pumpkin, eggs, granulated sugar, brown sugar, butter, cinnamon, nutmeg, and salt in another bowl. Stir this mixture into the milk-bagel mixture. Pour it all into the prepared baking dish.

Sprinkle the pudding with the raisins, then stir lightly to push the raisins down into the pudding—they could burn if too exposed. Sprinkle the pudding with the diced apple and the pecans.

Bake for 40 to 50 minutes, until the pudding is set and the pecans are toasty brown. Serve warm.

My School Lunch Cream Puff

Makes 12 medium cream puffs

or thirteen years, I attended the same tiny rural school, and for all that time, cream puffs reigned as the favorite school lunch dessert. Pale and somewhat underbaked, the puffs were filled with instant vanilla pudding, but we loved them nonetheless. To my adult taste buds, vanilla pudding seems downright pathetic. And pastry cream usually strikes me as gelatinous and bland. Rich puddings didn't have the oomph I wanted, and even the best custards weren't satisfying here—they oozed. Finally I hit upon this perfect filling—fluffy, rich, sweet, and stable.

Serve the puffs dusted with confectioners' sugar or drizzled with Rich Chocolate Sauce (page 125).

FLUFFY VANILLA FILLING
2 envelopes unflavored gelatine
1 vanilla bean
1 cup sugar
4 large egg yolks
1¼ cups heavy cream

PUFFS
8 tablespoons (1 stick) unsalted butter, cut into pieces
¼ teaspoon salt
1 cup all-purpose flour
4 large eggs

Sprinkle the gelatine over 1 cup water in a saucepan and allow it to soften for 5 minutes.

Split the vanilla bean lengthwise with a paring knife and scrape the tiny seeds into the pan. Add the bean pod. Whisk in ¾ cup of the sugar and the egg yolks. Cook the mixture over medium-low heat, stirring constantly with a rubber spatula and watching it carefully so that it doesn't boil. When it is steaming and somewhat thickened, remove it from the heat and strain it through a fine-mesh strainer.

Refrigerate the mixture, uncovered, stirring often. You want the gelatine to reach the softly-set stage—about as thick as pudding—but no further. It will take about 30 minutes.

When the gelatine has reached the right consistency, whip the cream with the remaining ¼ cup sugar until the cream forms very soft peaks. Fold the whipped cream into the gelatin mixture, combining the two well.

Cover the filling, return it to the refrigerator, and chill it for at least 2 hours, or as long as 2 days.

When ready to make the puffs, preheat your oven to 425°F.

Bring the butter, salt, and 1 cup water to a boil in a saucepan, stirring occasionally to melt the butter. Stir in the flour and continue to stir until the mixture comes away from the sides of the pan and forms a cohesive mass. Remove the pan from the heat and allow the dough to cool for 5 minutes. Beat the eggs into the dough, one at a time.

Spoon or pipe the dough onto an ungreased baking sheet, making 6 round puffs. Put the puffs in the oven and lower the temperature to 375°F. Bake until the puffs are golden and dry, 25 to 35 minutes, then cool them on a rack.

To assemble the cream puffs, slice off the tops of the puffs, remove any extra dough from inside each puff, if desired, and spoon the filling into the puffs. Alternatively, use a pastry bag with a sharp tip to pierce the bottom of the puffs and fill them without slicing their tops off.

Extra Cinnamon Bubble Bread

Serves 6 to 8

love cinnamon rolls and sticky buns and all those sorts of things, so I wondered, why can't I make a particularly rich version of such a bread—replete with caramel gooeyness and fall-apart structure—and serve it for dessert? So I did. That's the kind of guy I am.

Serve on a dessert plate drizzled with some Crème Anglaise (page 127).

1⅛ teaspoons yeast (half a packet)
2 large egg yolks
3 tablespoons unsalted butter, softened nearly to
   melting point in microwave
¼ cup plus 1 tablespoon packed light brown sugar
¾ teaspoon salt
1½ cups all-purpose flour, plus more as needed
½ cup heavy cream
½ cup currants or raisins
½ cup sliced almonds
½ cup sugar
4 to 6 teaspoons cinnamon, to taste

Dissolve the yeast in ½ cup warm water in a medium bowl. Whisk in the egg yolks, butter, 2 tablespoons of the brown sugar, and the salt. Add about half of the flour and stir the mixture until it is smooth. Stir in the rest of the flour—or as much as is needed to make a very soft but kneadable dough.

On a floured surface, knead the dough until it is smooth and elastic, about 5 minutes. Put the dough in a vegetable shortening-greased bowl and turn the dough to coat it with shortening. Cover the dough and let it rise in a warm place until doubled in size, 75 to 90 minutes.

Punch the dough down and turn it out onto a lightly floured surface.

Butter a 9 × 5-inch loaf pan. Spread the remaining 3 tablespoons brown sugar in the pan and pour in the cream. Next, stir together the currants, almonds, granulated sugar, and cinnamon in a medium bowl. Now pinch off small pieces of the dough and toss the pieces in the bowl with the currant/sugar mixture. When all the dough has been made into sugar-coated pieces, turn everything into the loaf pan, distributing the pieces relatively evenly. Cover the loaf pan and let it rise again until doubled, about 60 minutes. You can speed up this rising by warming the cream before you add it to the loaf pan. The bread should puff up and nearly fill the pan.

Near the end of the rising, preheat your oven to 375°F.

Bake the bubble bread for 22 to 26 minutes, until it is well browned and somewhat hollow sounding when tapped on top. Serve warm or at room temperature.

Almond-Apricot Mini-Soufflés

Serves 6

I wasn't prepared for the intensity and boldness of the flavor in these soufflés, so I decided to make them smaller than usual. They puff up beautifully and make a great presentation. They need to be served right out of the oven, so you do need to get the timing just right. But success is sweet. And pretty.

Sugar, for coating the dishes
¼ cup apricot preserves
3 tablespoons dried apricots (about ¾ ounce; see Note)
2 tablespoons almond paste
½ teaspoon pure vanilla extract
Small pinch of salt
3 large eggs, separated
¼ plus ⅛ teaspoon cream of tartar
1 tablespoon packed light brown sugar

Preheat your oven to 375°F. Butter six 4-ounce soufflé dishes or straight-sided ramekins. Coat the insides of the dishes with sugar, knocking out any excess sugar. Set a pot of water on to boil.

Puree the preserves, apricots, almond paste, vanilla, salt, and 1 tablespoon water in a food processor. Scrape down the bowl a couple of times if necessary. The goal is a paste with small bits of apricot still clearly visible.

With an electric mixer, beat the egg whites and cream of tartar on medium speed in a large bowl until frothy. Increase the speed to high and slowly add the brown sugar, beating until the whites form soft peaks.

Beat the egg yolks in another bowl until they are pale yellow, 1 to 2 minutes. Stir in the almond-apricot mixture. Now, working quickly but gently, fold in the beaten egg whites. Stop folding as soon as the mixture is nearly uniform.

Gently spoon the mixture into the prepared soufflé dishes. Set the dishes in a large baking dish or roasting pan. Carefully pour enough boiling water into the pan to reach halfway up the sides of the soufflé dishes.

Bake the soufflés for 12 to 18 minutes, until they are well browned on top and not particularly wobbly when shaken. Serve immediately.

Note: I usually buy unsulphured organic dried fruit, but the commercial dried apricots in the supermarkets that are labeled "California" apricots (as opposed to Turkish) are extremely flavorful and intense. They suit this recipe well.

BASIC RECIPES

....

he building blocks of dessert glory, the foundations of dessert fame, the final touches, the *sine qua non*.

Easy Tart Dough

Makes one 9-inch tart shell

found this tasty and forgiving tart dough in David Lebovitz's *Room for Dessert*, and I've relied on it ever since. No fussing with pastry cutters or adding just the right amount of water. No lugging out the food processor.

Even if you're making only one tart, you might want to double or triple the recipe, since the tightly wrapped dough keeps well in the refrigerator for several days, or for up to a month in the freezer.

6 tablespoons (¾ stick) unsalted butter, softened
¼ cup sugar
1 large egg yolk
1 cup all-purpose flour
⅛ teaspoon salt

With a hand mixer, beat the butter and sugar in a mixing bowl on low speed for 1 minute. Add the egg yolk and mix for another 30 seconds. It's okay if the mixture looks curdled.

Whisk the flour and salt together in another bowl to distribute the salt evenly. Add the flour mixture to the butter-egg mixture and beat on high speed until the dough clumps together into very large clumps and is smooth and holds together when pressed. Be patient: this could take a few minutes.

Form the dough into a disk about 1 inch thick and wrap it securely in plastic wrap. Chill it for at least 30 minutes.

If the dough is too stiff when it's time to roll it out, let it sit at room temperature for 5 minutes or so. Roll out the dough on a lightly floured work surface to an 11-inch circle until it is large enough to line your tart pan. Ease the dough into the tart pan and gently press it into the crease where the sides of the pan meet the bottom. Then gently press the dough against the sides of the pan. Roll your rolling pin over the top of the tart pan to shear off any excess dough. If there are any cracks in the dough, especially where the sides meet the bottom, patch it with the excess dough. Chill the tart shell for 20 minutes.

If you want to bake the dough before filling it, preheat your oven to 375°F. Line the chilled dough with aluminum foil and fill the foil with a thin layer of dried beans or rice. Bake the shell for 10 minutes, then gently remove the aluminum foil and beans and bake for another 8 to 10 minutes, until the edges are lightly browned. Let the crust cool before filling.

Occasionally, a recipe will call for a tart shell that's only partially baked, in which case, bake the crust for only about 10 minutes.

Galette Dough

Makes one 9-inch galette shell

he apple cider lends this flaky pastry tenderness and a pleasant tanginess that's particularly well suited to my Apple Galette (page 55). The wrapped dough can be refrigerated for 3 days or frozen for a month. This dough also makes a good traditional tart crust or piecrust.

1¼ cups all-purpose flour
1 teaspoon sugar
½ teaspoon salt
8 tablespoons (1 stick) unsalted butter, cold, cut into
    pieces
1¼ teaspoons apple cider vinegar, stirred into
    6 tablespoons ice water

Pulse the flour, sugar, and salt briefly in the food processor. Add the butter and pulse until the pieces of butter are about the size of peas. While pulsing, drizzle in the apple cider vinegar and water. Stop the machine when the dough starts to clump together. It's okay if the dough is wet. The dough may take more or less water than called for.

Alternatively, if you want to use your hands instead of a food processor, stir the flour, sugar, and salt together in a bowl. Add the butter and cut it in with a pastry blender until the mixture is mealy and crumbly. Gradually sprinkle in the apple cider and water while stirring and tossing the mixture with a fork, stirring just until the dough comes together.

Form the dough into a disk 1 inch thick and wrap it securely in plastic wrap. Chill the dough for at least 1 hour.

When you're ready to roll out the dough, remove it from the refrigerator and let it sit at room temperature until it is pliable enough to work with—anywhere from 5 to 15 minutes.

If you're making my Apple Galette, turn to page 55 and follow the instructions there. If you're following a different recipe, roll out the dough to the desired size. Fit it into the tart pan, if you're using one. Chill the rolled-out dough for at least 30 minutes before baking.

If you want to prebake the empty shell in a tart pan, preheat your oven to 375°F. Line the shell with aluminum foil and weight it down with dried beans or rice. Bake for 15 minutes, then remove the foil and weights and bake for another 5 to 10 minutes, until the sides are lightly browned and the bottom is dry to the touch. Cool the shell completely before filling.

Occasionally, a recipe will call for a tart shell that's only partially baked, in which case bake the crust for only about 10 minutes.

Shortening Piecrust

Makes one 9-inch piecrust

n college, the first pies I made by myself were shortening based, and somehow even I managed to turn out a flaky crust. Ten years and many piecrusts later, I still often prefer the remarkable flakiness of a shortening piecrust. True, this crust doesn't have the flavor that a good butter crust does (see page 122), but most pie fillings overshadow the flavor of the piecrust anyway. It's a hassle to measure out half a cup of shortening, so I buy those premeasured sticks of shortening.

1½ cups all-purpose flour
½ teaspoon salt
½ cup vegetable shortening
¼ cup ice water, more or less

Stir together the flour and salt in a bowl. With a pastry blender, cut in the shortening until the mixture is crumbly and uniform, with a few pea-sized bits of shortening still visible. Slowly sprinkle the water over the mixture, tossing and stirring everything with a fork. When the mixture is well moistened and clumps together easily, gather it into a ball, then flatten it into a disk. Don't be scared about adding too much water—the dough should be moist, not dry and crumbly. Wrap the disk well in plastic wrap and refrigerate it for at least 30 minutes, or for as long as 24 hours.

If the chilled dough is too hard when it's time to roll it out, let it stand at room temperature for several minutes. Roll the dough out to a 12-inch round on a floured work surface—or on a well-floured piece of parchment paper, which makes handling the dough easier. Carefully transfer the dough crust to the pie plate and softly press it against the sides of the pan and into the seam where the sides meet the bottom. Flute the edge of the crust.

To prebake the pie shell, preheat your oven to 400°F. Prick the bottom of the crust with the tines of a fork. Line the pan with aluminum foil, then weight the foil with dried beans or rice. Bake the crust for 12 to 16 minutes, until it is nicely browned. For a well-browned bottom crust, you can remove the foil and weights after about 8 minutes of baking, then continue baking. Let the pie shell cool before filling.

Double-Crust Shortening Piecrust

Follow the directions above, using 2¼ cups flour, ¾ teaspoon salt, ¾ cup vegetable shortening, and 6 tablespoons ice water.

Butter Piecrust

Makes one 9-inch piecrust

For the best flavor, go with a butter-based pastry crust.

1 cup plus 1 tablespoon all-purpose flour
¼ teaspoon salt
8 tablespoons (1 stick) unsalted butter, chilled and cut into pieces
3 tablespoons ice water, more or less

Stir together the flour and salt in a bowl. With a pastry blender, cut in the butter until the mixture is crumbly and uniform, with a few pea-sized bits of butter still visible. Slowly sprinkle the water over the mixture, tossing and stirring everything with a fork. When the mixture is well moistened and clumps together easily, gather it into a ball, then flatten it into a disk. You can roll out the dough immediately or chill it wrapped well in plastic wrap for up to 24 hours.

If the chilled dough is too hard when it's time to roll it out, let it stand at room temperature for several minutes. Roll the dough out on a floured work surface—or on a well-floured piece of parchment paper, which makes handling the dough easier. Carefully transfer the dough to the pie plate and softly press it against the sides of the pan and into the seam where the sides meet the bottom. Flute the edge of the crust.

To prebake the pie shell, preheat your oven to 400°F. Prick the bottom of the crust with the tines of a fork. Line the pan with aluminum foil, then weight the foil with dried beans or rice. Bake the piecrust for 12 to 16 minutes, until it is nicely browned. For a well-browned bottom crust, you can remove the foil and weights after about 8 minutes of baking, then continue baking. Let the pie shell cool before filling.

Double-Crust Butter Piecrust

Follow the directions above, using 2 cups flour, ½ teaspoon salt, ½ pound (2 sticks) butter, and ¼ cup plus 2 tablespoons ice water.

Graham Cracker Crumb Piecrust

Makes one 9-inch piecrust

for those pies that need this crumbly-salty-sweet classic, such as chiffon pies or cheesecakey-type pies. Or, heck, just dump some chocolate pudding in one of these crusts and you've got an instant crowd pleaser. To make a similar crust in a 9-inch tart pan, halve the recipe.

1½ cups graham cracker crumbs (11 or 12 whole crackers)
6 tablespoons (¾ stick) unsalted butter, melted
¼ cup sugar
Pinch of salt

Stir all the ingredients together until combined. Press the mixture into the bottom and up the sides of a 9-inch pie plate, compacting the crumbs with the flat bottom of a glass if necessary. Refrigerate the crust until needed.

Rich Chocolate Sauce

Makes about 1 cup

The title says enough, doesn't it? Serve warm or at room temperature.

½ cup heavy cream
¼ cup light corn syrup
Pinch of salt
3 tablespoons unsalted butter, cut into pieces
4 ounces bittersweet chocolate, finely chopped

Whisk together the cream, corn syrup, and salt in a saucepan. Add the butter and bring to a boil. Remove from the heat, add the chocolate, cover the pan and let stand for 5 minutes. Then gently whisk the sauce until it's smooth.

Caramel Sauce

Makes about 1 cup

drizzle it over ice cream, spoon it over cake, swirl it into yogurt . . .

½ cup packed light brown sugar
¼ cup heavy cream
2 tablespoons light corn syrup
2 tablespoons unsalted butter
1 teaspoon pure vanilla extract

Combine all the ingredients in a small saucepan and bring to a boil over medium heat, stirring constantly. Boil the caramel for 2 minutes, then remove it from the heat.

Serve warm or at room temperature.

Crème Anglaise

Makes about 2½ cups

nectar of the gods, this timeless, luxurious, and always-perfect vanilla custard sauce is a welcome addition to all kinds of cakes, pies, and tarts. Use it wherever whipped cream or vanilla ice cream would be appropriate, or employ it as a decorative garnish on your dessert plates and watch your guests mop up every last drop. It can be refrigerated for up to 4 days.

2 cups milk
½ vanilla bean
¼ cup plus 2 tablespoons sugar
Pinch of salt
6 large egg yolks

Pour the milk into a medium saucepan. Split the vanilla bean in half and scrape the tiny seeds into the milk. Add the vanilla bean pod, as well as the sugar and salt. Heat the mixture over medium heat, stirring until the sugar dissolves, just until small bubbles begin to rise.

While the milk heats up, prepare an ice bath by filling a big bowl with water and ice and nesting another bowl—preferably metal—in the water. When the milk bubbles, remove it from the heat.

Whisk the egg yolks in another bowl. Drizzle a bit of the hot milk into the yolks, whisking constantly, then pour the yolks into the saucepan. Return the pan to medium heat and stir, frequently scraping the bottom of the pan, until the mixture thickens to approximately the consistency of heavy cream, about 2 minutes.

Remove the pan from the heat and strain the custard into the bowl nestled in the ice water. Stir the crème anglaise for a couple of minutes as it cools, then cover it and refrigerate it until needed.

Cheater's Crème Anglaise

Well, this is a bit childish, but it works. For a last-minute crème anglaise, substitute melted premium vanilla ice cream.

Sweetened Whipped Cream

Makes about 2 cups

I've been served desserts in top-notch restaurants where the whipped cream was actually better than the dessert. That's a commentary on both the mediocrity of many restaurant desserts and the ever-satisfying qualities of whipped cream. Though we're all enamored of sweetened whipped cream, some desserts are particularly good when accompanied by *unsweetened* whipped cream. Try it sometime. Remember, pasteurized cream tastes better than ultrapasteurized cream.

1 cup heavy cream
1 tablespoon sugar, or to taste
½ teaspoon pure vanilla extract, or to taste, optional

For best results, put your bowl and your beaters (or whisk) in the freezer for at least 30 minutes before you want to whip the cream.

With an electric mixer or whisk, whip the cream until it starts to gain body. Then add the sugar and vanilla, if desired, and continue whipping. Whip until the cream is softly set and billowy. Serve immediately or cover and refrigerate for up to 2 hours.

If the cream begins to separate before you can serve it, rewhip it briefly.

Raspberry Coulis

Makes about 2½ cups

his ubiquitous sauce is perfect with ice creams, cakes, and some custards. Sometimes I wish it were served in a cup with a straw.

3 cups fresh raspberries
⅓ cup sugar, or to taste
½ teaspoon fresh lemon juice, or to taste

Puree the raspberries along with about half of the sugar in the food processor. Taste the puree and add more sugar and the lemon juice as needed. If the puree is too thick, add a few tablespoons of water. Pulse to mix, and readjust the sugar and lemon juice.

When the puree tastes right, strain it through a fine-mesh strainer to remove the seeds. Refrigerate it for up to 3 days.

Note: Frozen raspberries make a fine coulis. Thaw 20 ounces (2 packages) of raspberries in the refrigerator overnight; strain and reserve their juices. Then proceed as above, using the reserved juices to thin the coulis, if desired.

Blackberry Coulis

Follow the above recipe, substituting blackberries, but increase the sugar to about ½ cup.

Jam Glaze

Makes about ⅓ cup

¼ **cup jam, any flavor**
2 tablespoons water

Let the jam melt in the water in a saucepan over medium heat. Strain the jam, then put it back in the pan and bring it to a boil. Let the glaze cool slightly, then spread it over a cooled cake.

Chocolate Ganache

Makes about 1½ cups

drizzle it on cakes or ice creams for a pure chocolate punch. It keeps for days refrigerated.

8 ounces bittersweet chocolate, in pieces
1 cup heavy cream

Put the chocolate in a food processor and process until the chocolate is fine. Transfer the chocolate to a bowl.

Heat the cream over medium heat until it boils, watching it very carefully to avoid a boilover.

Pour the cream over the chocolate. Let the mixture sit for a few minutes, then stir it slowly until the ganache is smooth. Let the ganache cool until it's the right consistency for your purposes. The cooler the ganache gets, the thicker it becomes. For spreading on a cake (such as Indispensable Chocolate Torte, page 66), you want the ganache to be slightly warmer than room temperature.

DESSERT FINDER

ntense Desserts

esserts with Elegant Simplicity

h omey and Comforting Desserts

l ast-Minute Desserts

d esserts That Make a Visual Impression

Chocolate Desserts

Low- and No-Fat Desserts

Desserts for the Beginning Baker

SOURCES

AMERICAN SPOON FOODS
P.O. Box 566
Petoskey, MI 49770-0566
888-735-6700
www.spoon.com

A source for black walnuts, dried blueberries, dried tart cherries, maple syrup, honey, and home-canned preserves and berries.

THE BAKER'S CATALOGUE
P.O. Box 876
Norwich, VT 05055-0876
800-827-6836
www.bakerscatalogue.com

A baker's paradise: a whole catalogue of bread-baking supplies, cake supplies, pastry supplies, as well as many ingredients—from Merckens bittersweet chocolate and Nielsen-Massey vanilla extract to Missouri black walnuts and a wide array of top-notch flours.

COOK'S ILLUSTRATED
www.cooksillustrated.com

My favorite cooking magazine. It eschews the flashy, faddish
approach of the big glossy magazines and instead offers a straightforward and common-sense approach to cooking. The recipes
work every time, and the unique format of the magazine gives you
insight into the recipe development process. A remarkable learning
tool for bakers and chefs of all skill levels.

PENZEYS SPICES
P.O. Box 933
Muskego, WI 53150
800-741-7787
www.penzeys.com

The one-stop source for spices, extracts, and vanilla beans.

SUR LA TABLE
P.O. Box 34707
Seattle WA 98124-1707
800-243-0852
www.surlatable.com

An excellent source for all kinds of tools and bakeware. Their catalogues are gorgeous, and they often have baking classes in their
stores.

SWEET CELEBRATIONS
P.O. Box 39426
Edina, MN 55439-0426
800-328-6722
www.sweetc.com

Formerly known as Maid of Scandinavia, a source for Callebaut unsweetened chocolate and Merckens chocolate, as well as a wide variety of cake-making supplies.

WILLIAMS-SONOMA
P.O. Box 7456
San Francisco, CA 94120-7456
800-541-2233
www.williams-sonoma.com

The grandaddy purveyor of high-quality kitchen tools, cookware, and tableware—available through beautiful catalogues, online, and in stores nationwide.

INDEX

milk, hot, sponge cake with citrus
   syrup, 68–70
mint leaf ice cream, 92–93
mocha mousse wafers, 84–85
molasses softies with candied
   ginger, 82–83
my school lunch cream puff, 109–10

nectarine and white chocolate ice
   cream, 94–95
Neufchâtel cheese, in berry brûlée,
   22–23

oatmeal blackberry pie, 57
oats, in chocolate-dipped ranger
   cookies, 78–79
orange:
   and chocolate chiffon pie, 47–48
   -drop cookies, 76–77
   in queen of puddings with
      cherries, 37–38
   sauce, slow-roasted, 24–25

peach(es):
   blueberries, almonds and, en
      papillote, 18–19
   pie with almond crumb topping,
      45–46
peanut butter and chocolate cake,
   71–72
pears, baked with pine nuts, dried
   cherries, and golden raisins,
   26

pecans, in apple-pumpkin bagel
   pudding, 107–8
piecrust:
   butter, 122–23
   double-crust butter, 122–23
   double-crust shortening,
      120–21
   graham cracker crumb, 124
   shortening, 120–21
pies and tarts, 43–58
   apple galette, 55–56
   blackberry oatmeal, 57
   black walnut and dried blueberry,
      49–50
   grapefruit-lime, with honey
      poppy seed whipped cream,
      53–54
   hanging-crust blueberry-
      blackberry cobbler, 51–52
   hanging-crust rhubarb cobbler,
      51–52
   maple custard, 44
   orange and chocolate chiffon,
      47–48
   peach, with almond crumb
      topping, 45–46
piloncillo:
   in slow-roasted orange sauce,
      24–25
   in slow-roasted pineapple sauce,
      24–25
pineapple:
   and kumquat salad, 27
   sauce, slow-roasted, 24–25
pine nuts, baked pears with dried
   cherries, golden raisins and,
   26
poppy seed(s):
   cake, whole wheat and, 64–65